Caspar David Friedrich: 110 Masterpieces

By Maria Tsaneva

First Edition

*****

Caspar David Friedrich: 110 Masterpieces
*****

Foreword

Caspar David Friedrich (1774 – 1840) was a 19th-century German Romantic landscape painter, generally considered the most important German artist of his generation and one of the most original geniuses in the history of landscape painting. He is best known for his mid-period allegorical landscapes which typically feature contemplative figures silhouetted against night skies, morning mists, barren trees or Gothic ruins. His primary interest as an artist was the contemplation of nature, and his often symbolic and anti-classical work seeks to convey a subjective, emotional response to the natural world. Friedrich's paintings characteristically set a human presence in diminished perspective amid expansive landscapes, reducing the figures to a scale that, according to the art historian Christopher John Murray, directs "the viewer's gaze towards their metaphysical dimension".

He was born at Greifswald on the Baltic coast, and after studying at the Copenhagen Academy with Juel and Abildgaard from 1794 to 1798, he settled permanently in Dresden. There he led a quiet life, interrupted only by occasional excursions to the mountains or the coast of Pomerania, pursuing with a rare and instinctive single-mindedness his personal insight into the spiritual significance of landscape. Caspar David Friedrich was intensely introspective and often melancholic and he relied on deep contemplation to summon up mentally the images he was to put on canvas. 'Close your bodily eye, so that you may see your picture first with your spiritual eye', he wrote, 'then bring to the light of day that which you have seen in the darkness so that it may react on others from the outside inwards.'

Friedrich began with topographical drawings in pencil and sepia wash and did not take up oil painting until 1807. One of his first works in the new medium, The Cross in the Mountains (Staatliche Kunstsammlungen, Dresden, 1808), caused great controversy because it was painted as an altarpiece, and to use a landscape in this unprecedented way was considered sacrilege by some critics. His choice of subjects often broke new ground and he discovered aspects of nature so far unseen: an infinite stretch of sea or mountains, snow-covered or fog-bound plains seen in the strange light of sunrise, dusk, or moonlight. He seldom uses obvious religious imagery, but his landscapes convey a sense of haunting spirituality.

Friedrich had a severe stroke in 1835 and returned to his small sepias. He was virtually forgotten at the time of his death and his immediate influence was confined to members of his circle in Dresden, notably Georg Friedrich Kersting, who sometimes painted the figures in Friedrich's work. It was only at the end of the 19th century, with the rise of Symbolism, that his greatness began to be recognized. Most of his work is still in Germany.

Paintings and Drawings

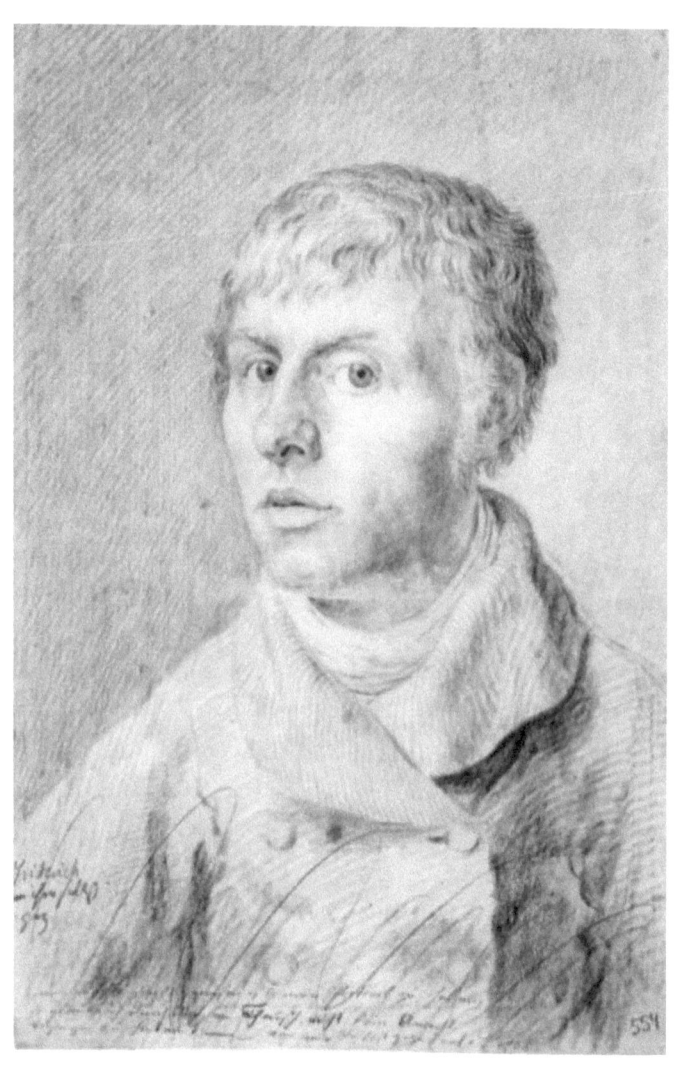

Self-portrait as a young man, 1800, drawing

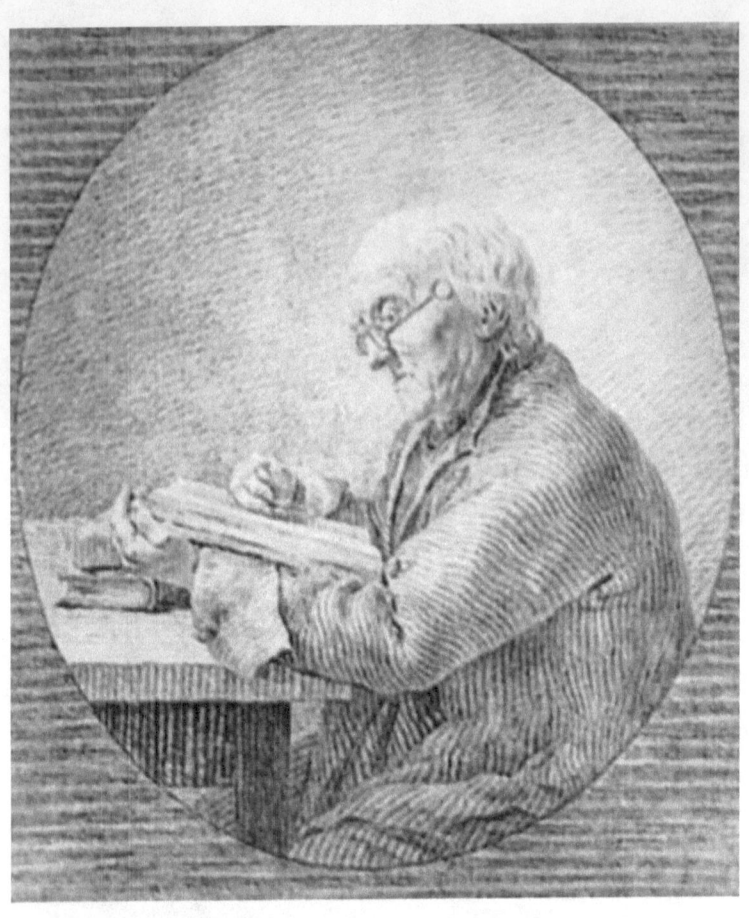

Adolf Gottlieb Friedrich, Reading, 1802, drawing

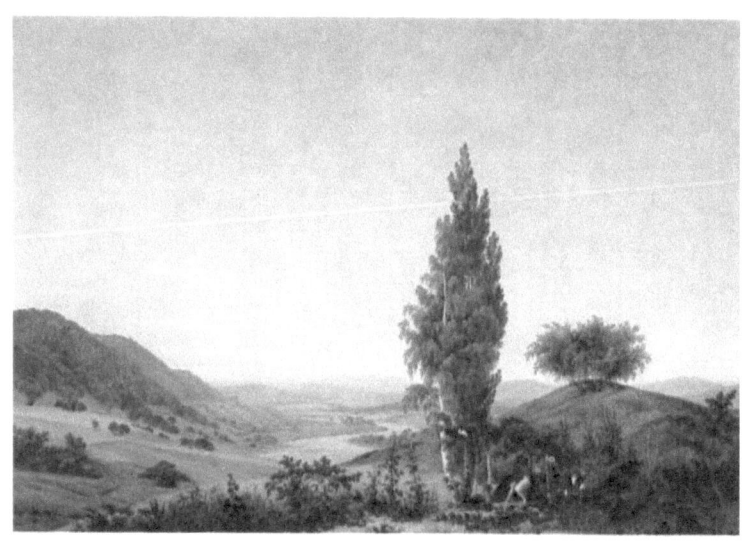

The summer, 1807, oil on canvas

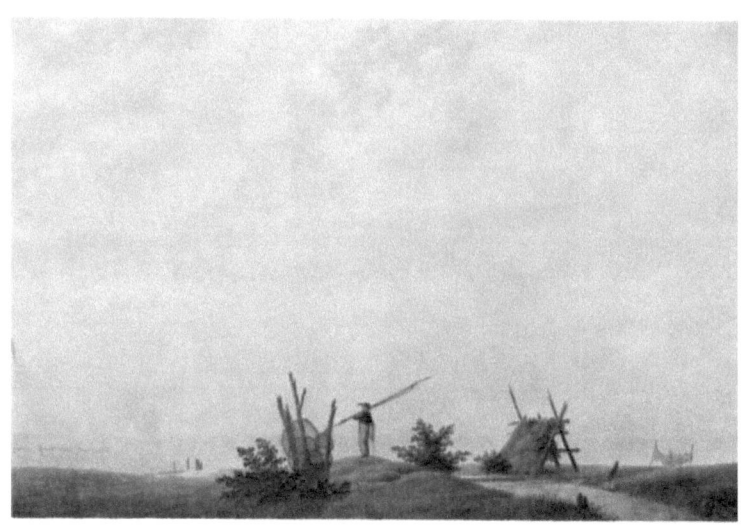

Sea beach with fisherman (The fisherman), 1807, oil on canvas

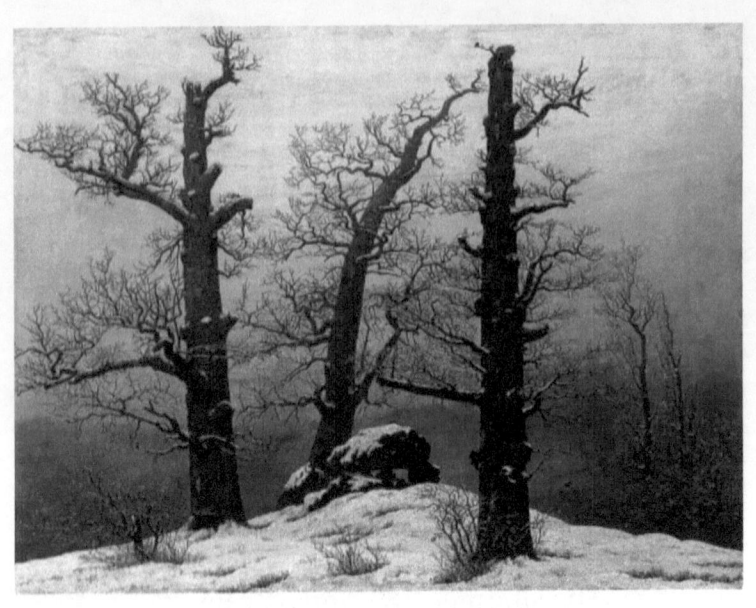

Dolmen in snow, 1807, oil on canvas

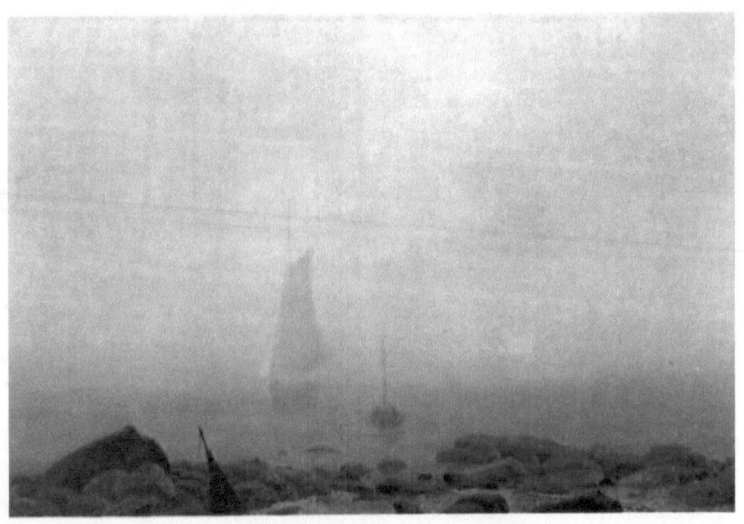

Fog, 1807, oil on canvas

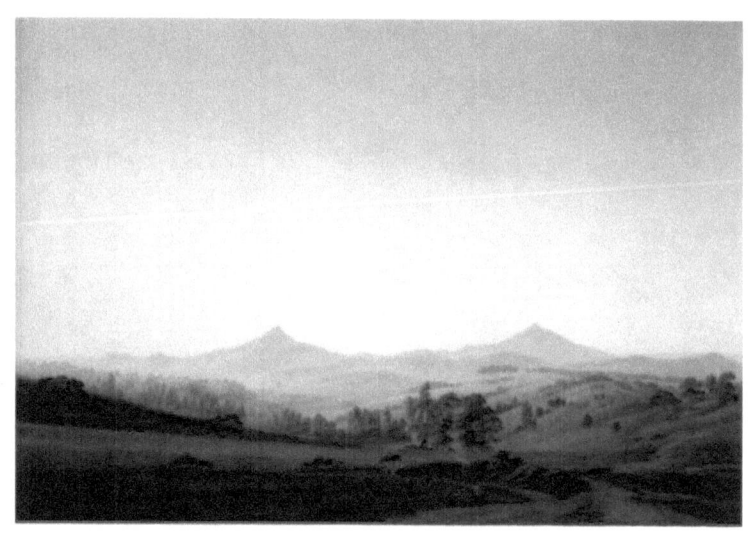

Bohemian Landscape with Mount Milleschauer, 1808,
oil on canvas

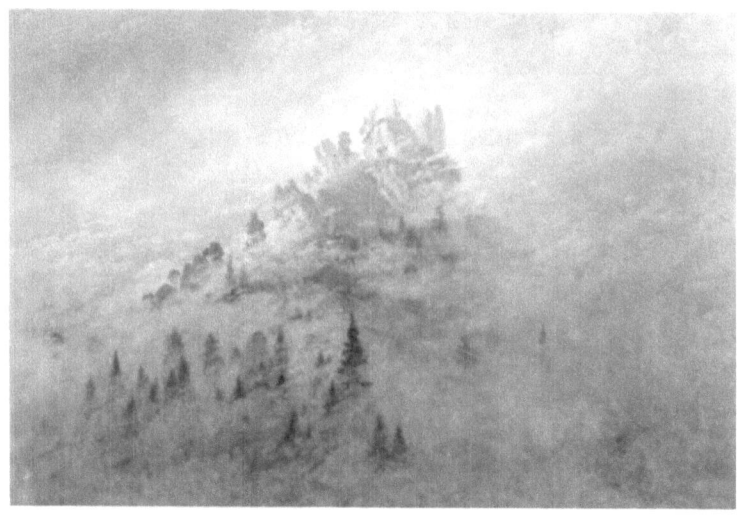

Morning mist in the mountains, 1808, oil on canvas

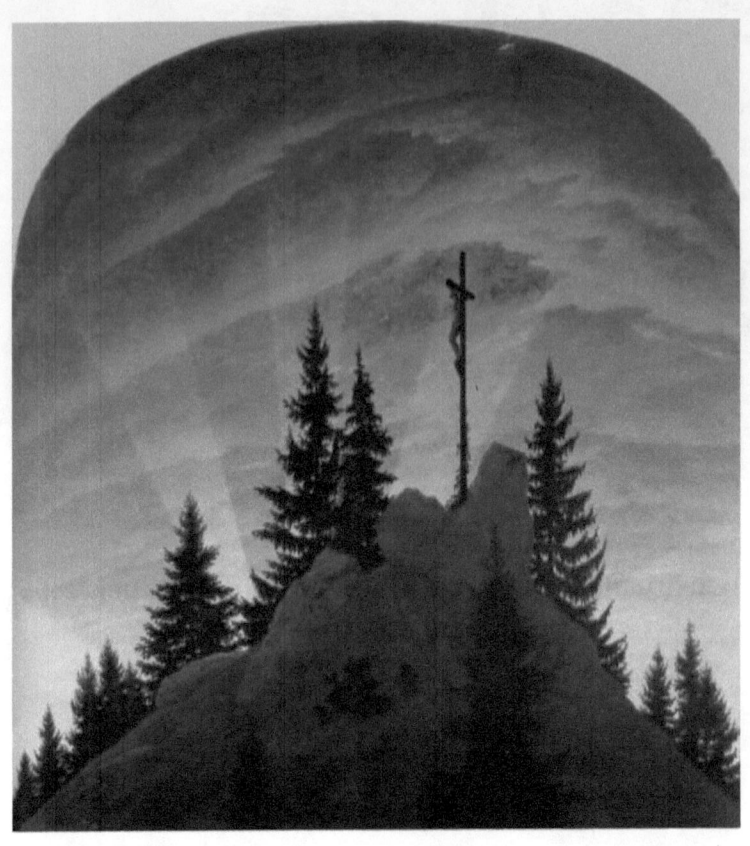

Cross in the Mountains (Tetschen Altar), 1808, oil on canvas

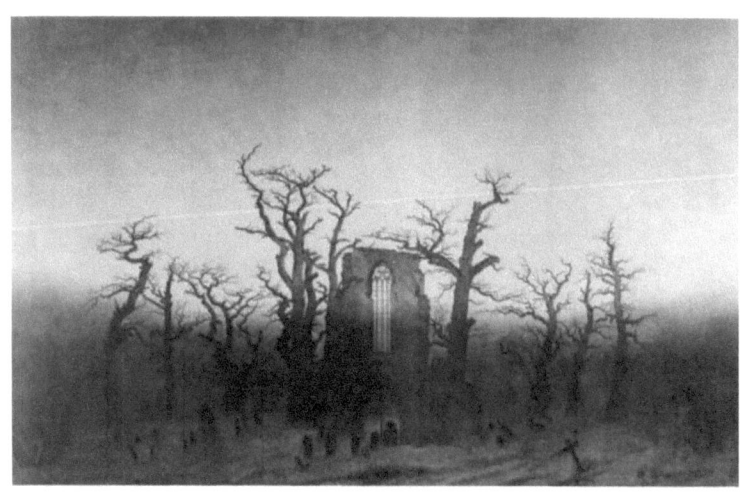

The Abbey in the Oakwood, 1810, oil on canvas

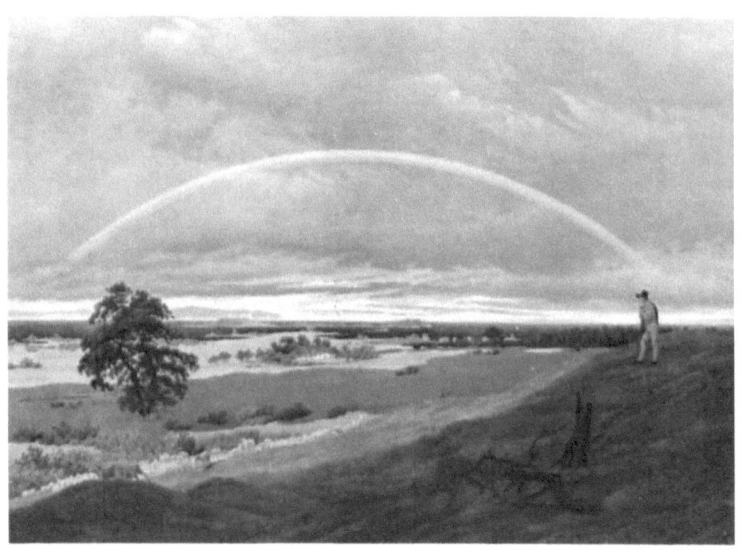

Landscape with rainbow, c.1810, oil on canvas

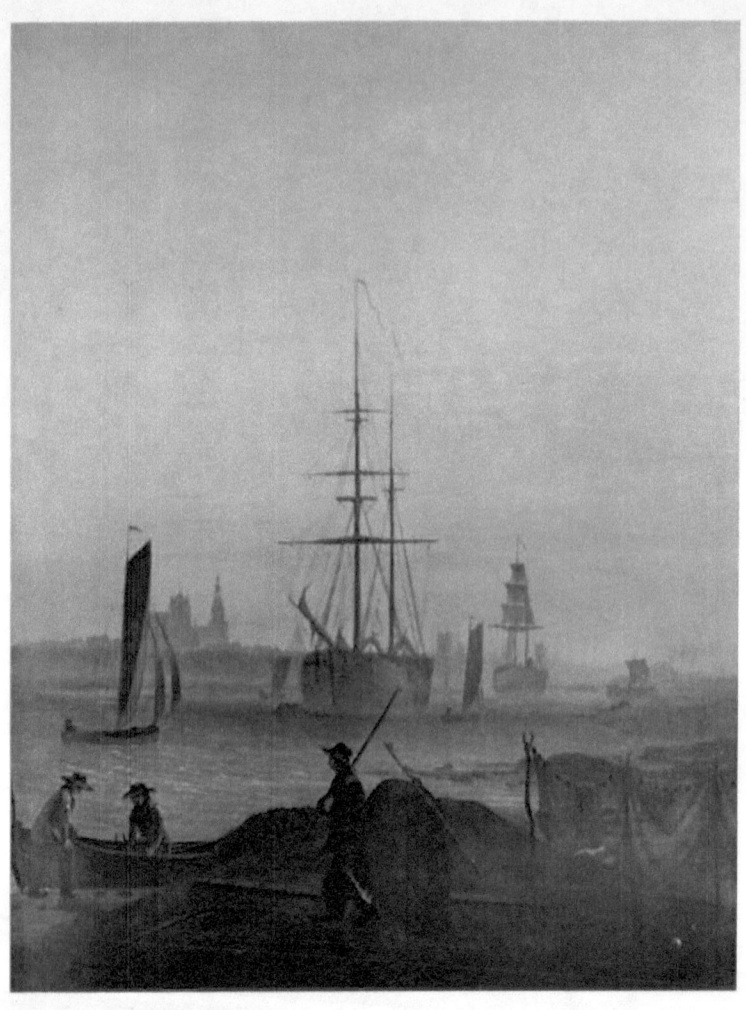

Ships at the port of Greifswald, c.1810, oil on canvas

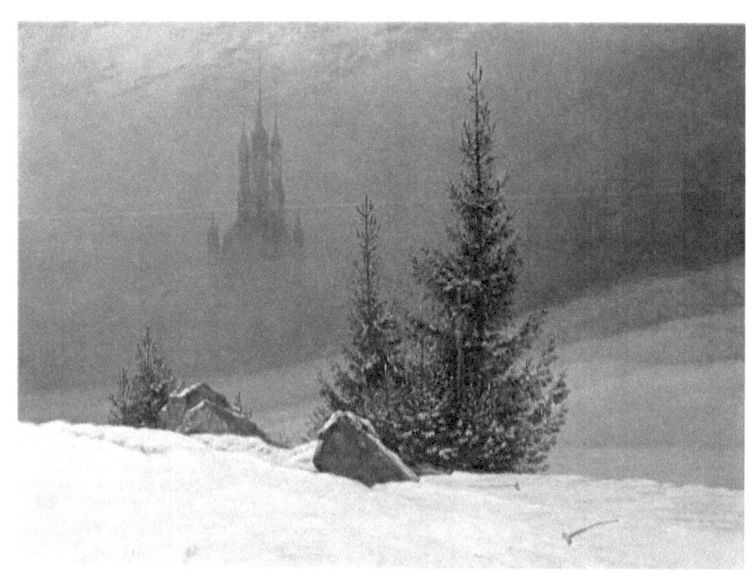

Winter landscape, c.1811, oil on canvas

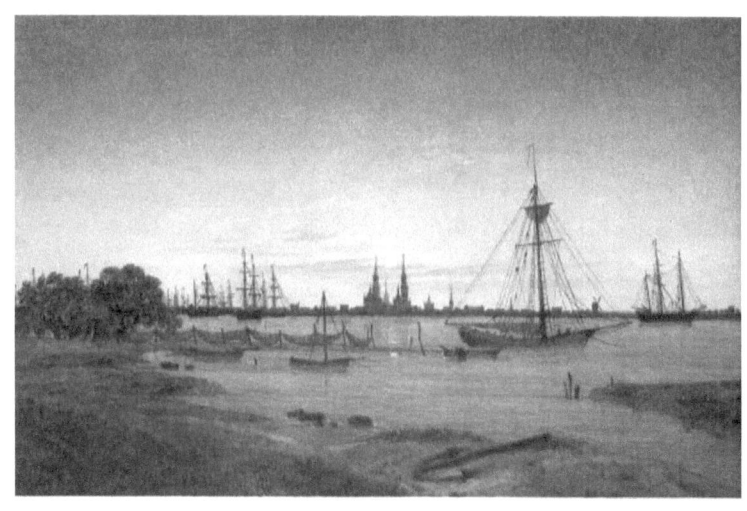

Port by Moonlight , 1811, oil on canvas

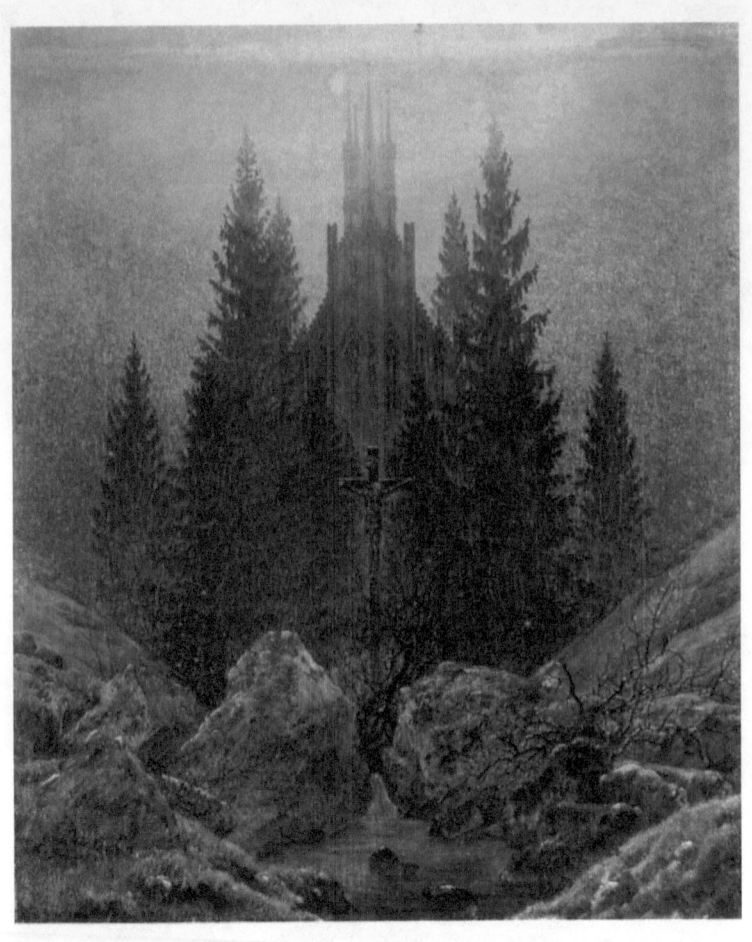

Cross and church in the mountains, 1812, oil on canvas

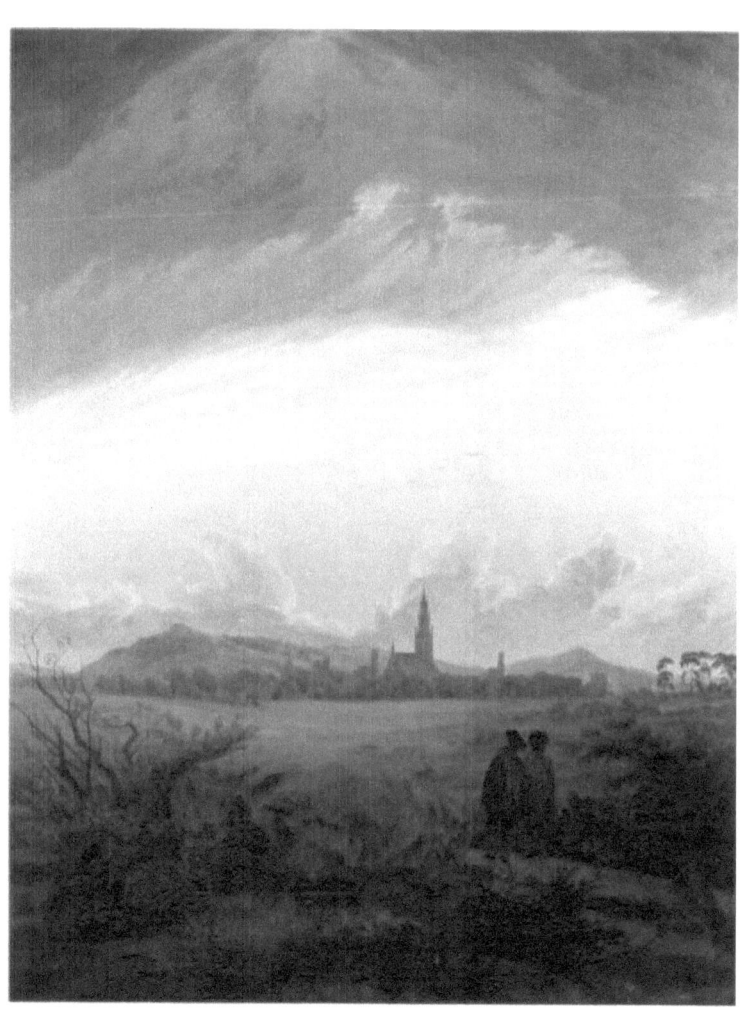

Neubrandenburg, c.1816-c.1817, oil on canvas

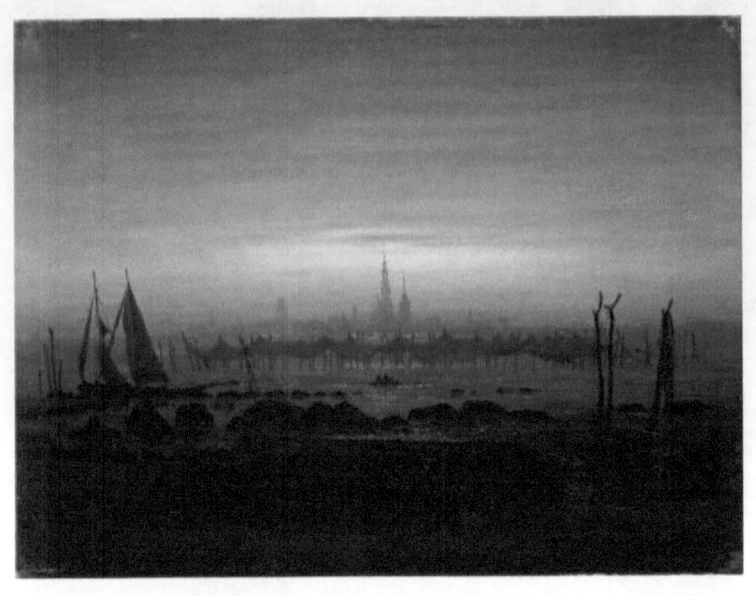

Greifswald in moonlight, 1817, oil on canvas

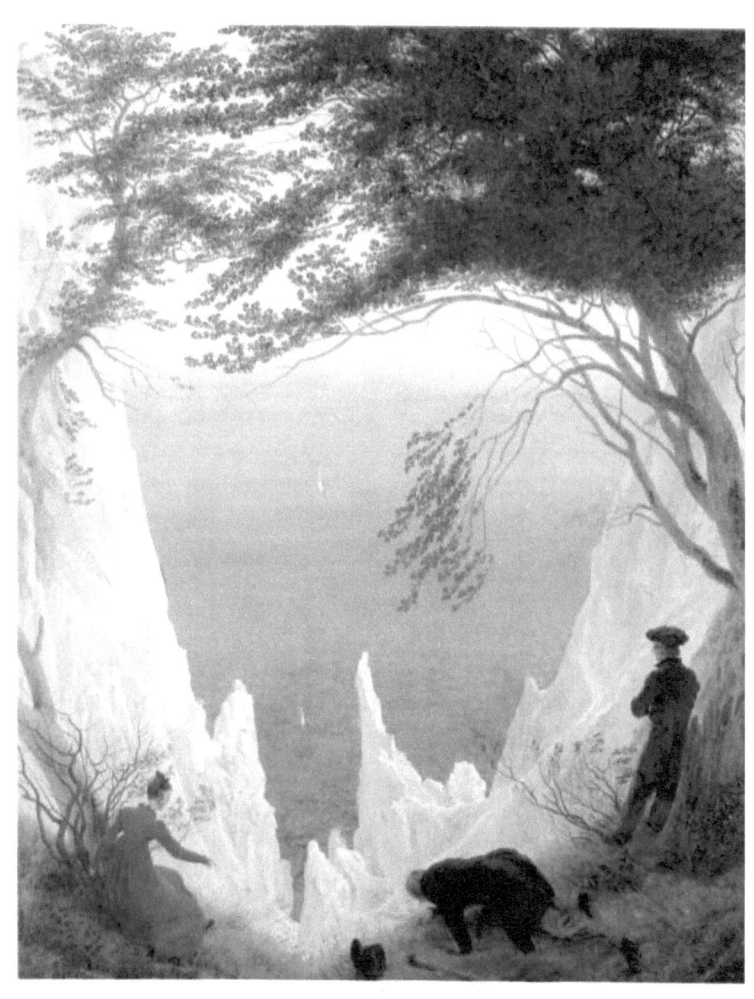

Chalk Cliffs on Rügen, c.1817, oil on canvas

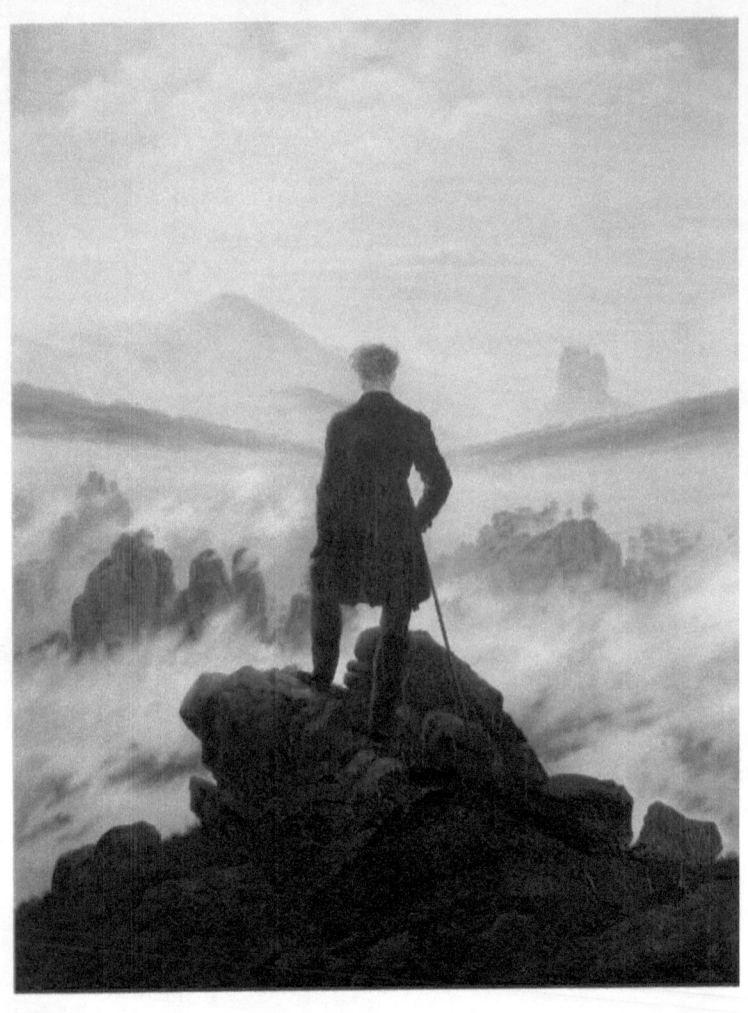

The wanderer above the sea of fog, 1818, oil on canvas

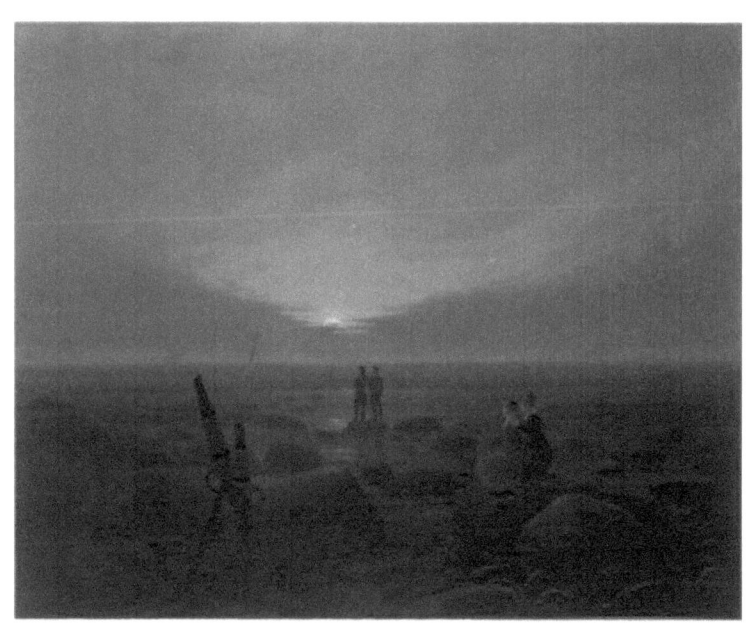

Twilight at seaside, 1819, oil on canvas

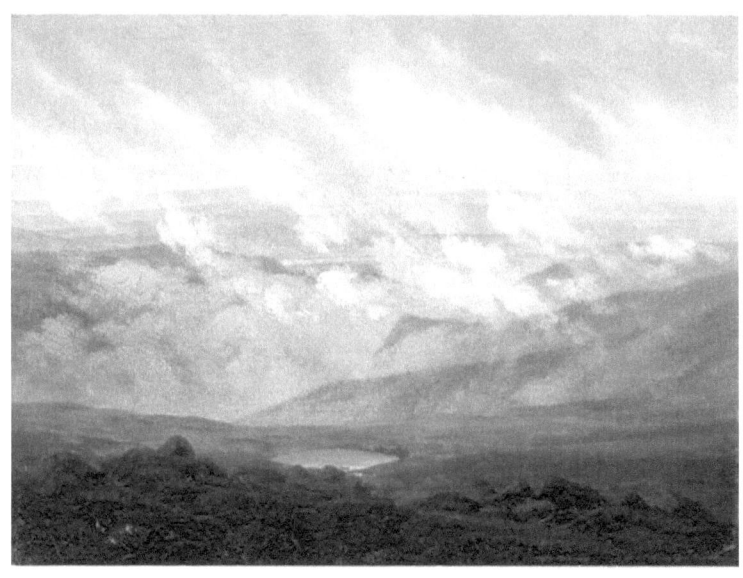

Drifting Clouds, 1820, oil on canvas

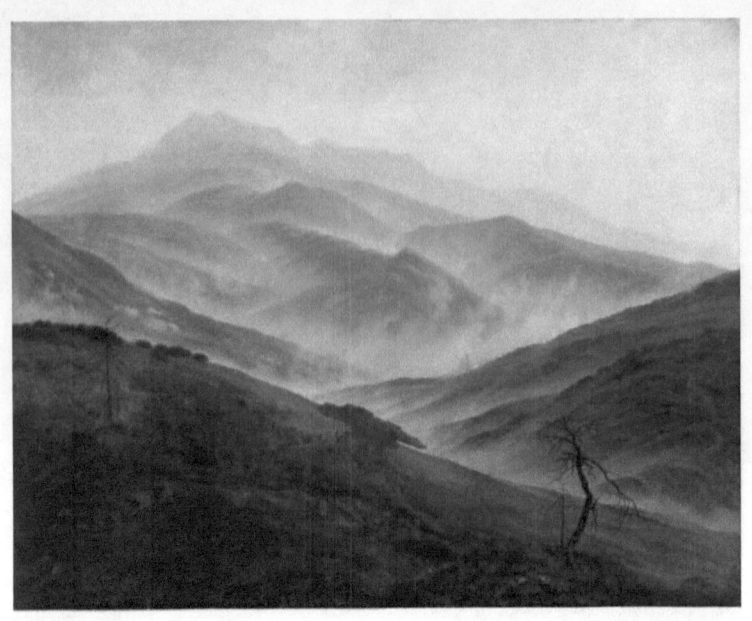

Giant Mountains Landscape with Rising Fog, 1820, oil on canvas

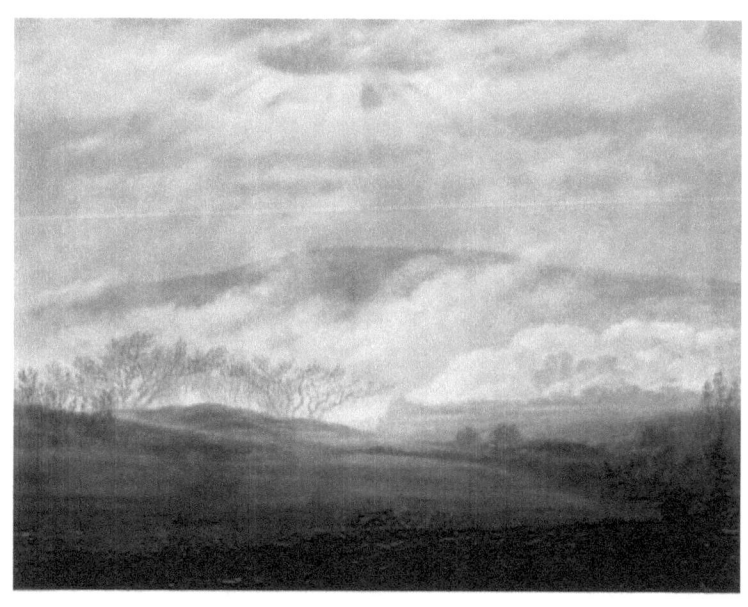

Fog in the Elbe Valley, 1821, oil on canvas

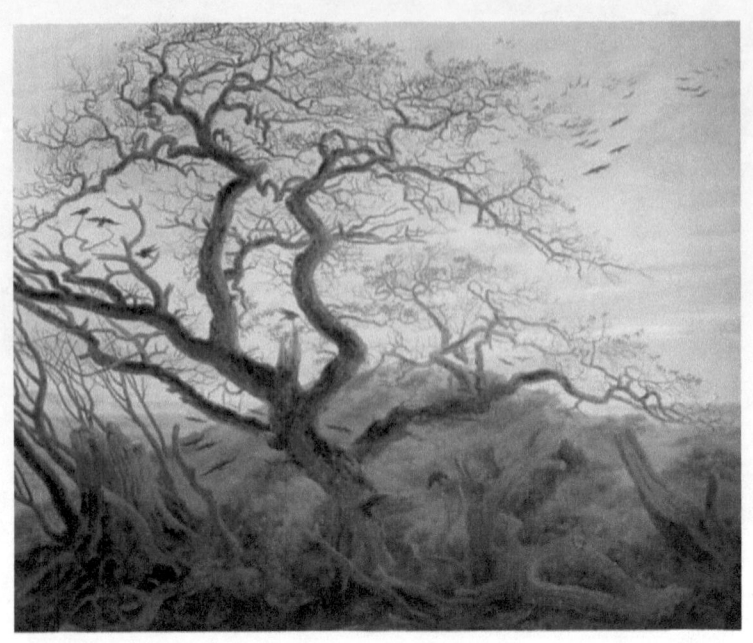

The Tree of Crows, 1822, oil on canvas

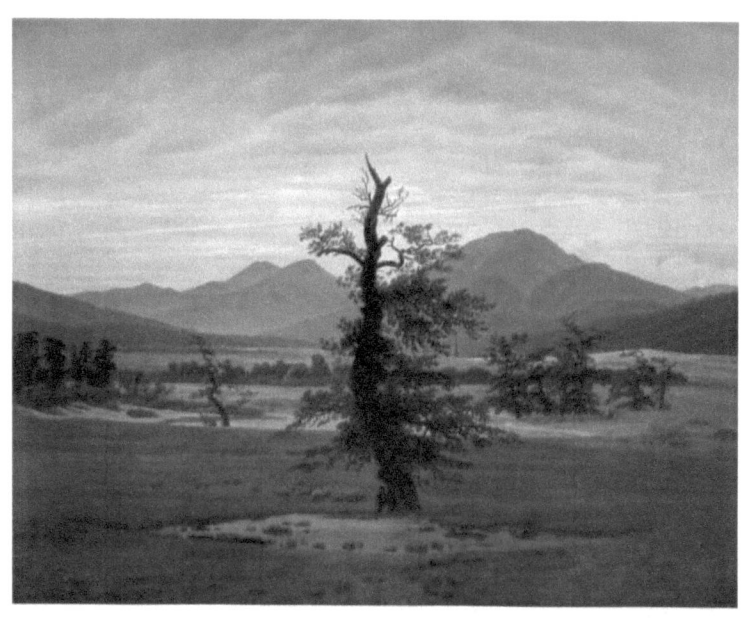

Solitary Tree, 1822, oil on canvas

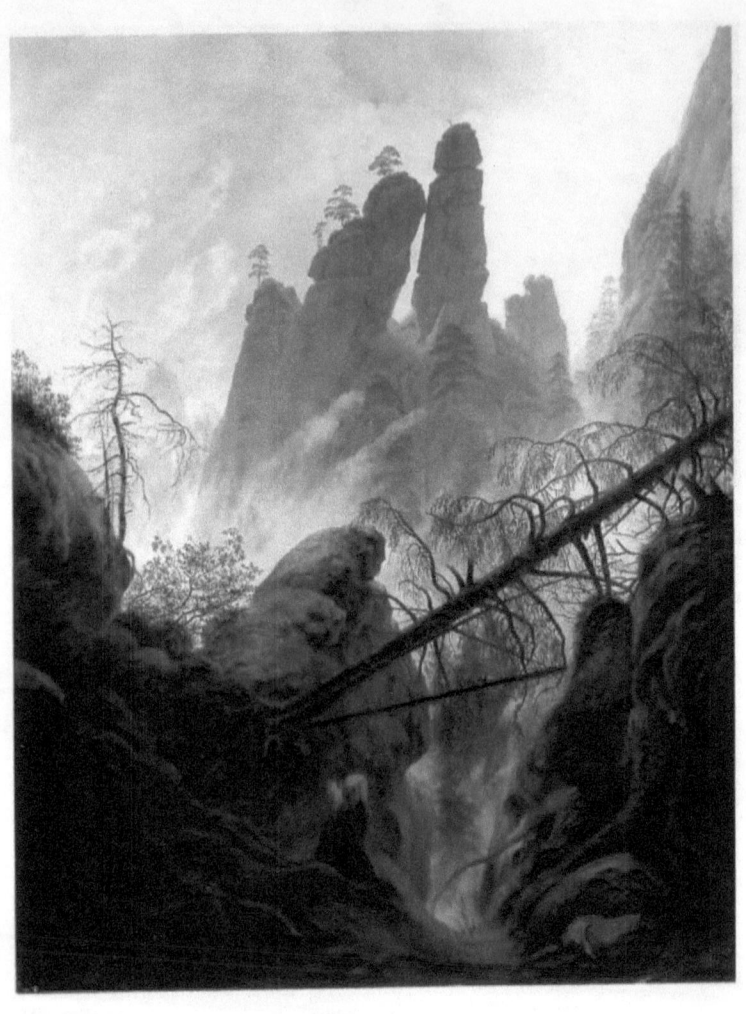

Rocky Ravine, 1823, oil on canvas

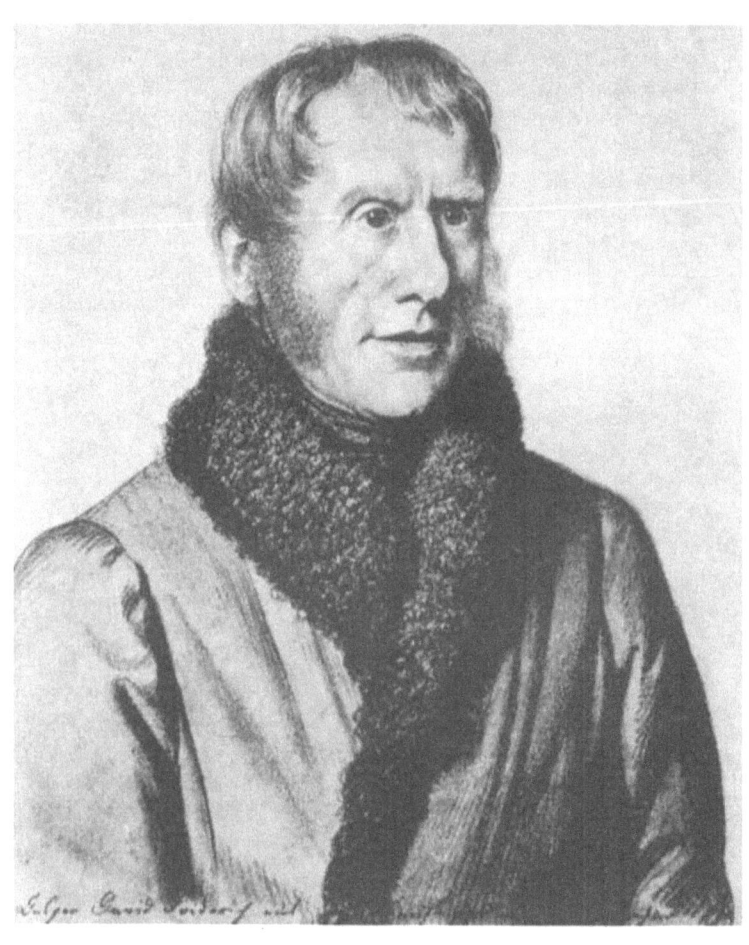

Carl Vogelvon Vogelstein, 1823, drawing

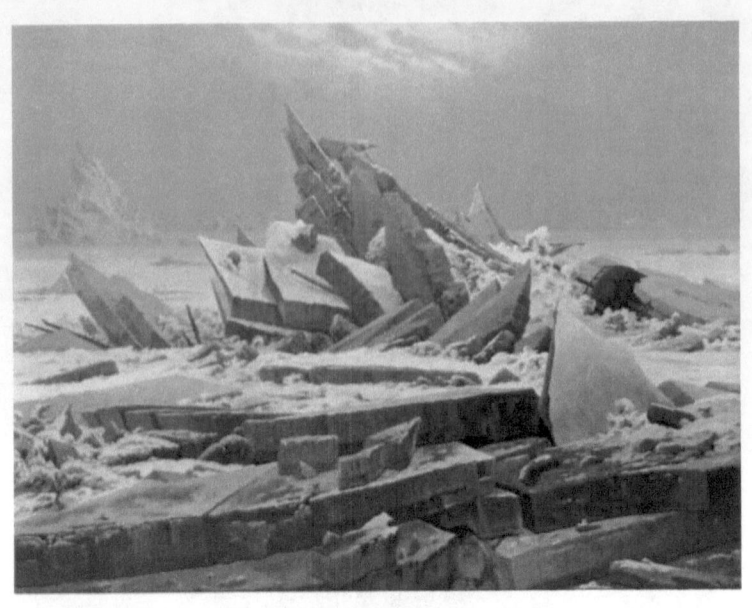

The Sea of Ice, 1823-1824, oil on canvas

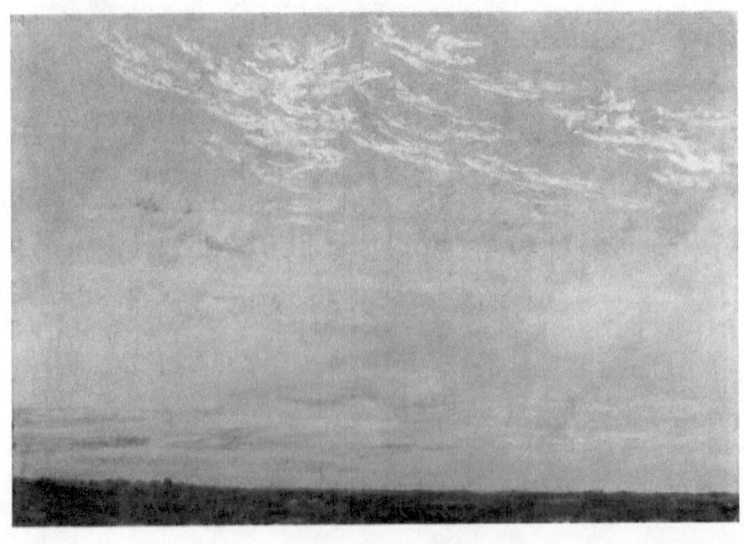

The Cemetery Entrance, 1825, oil on canvas

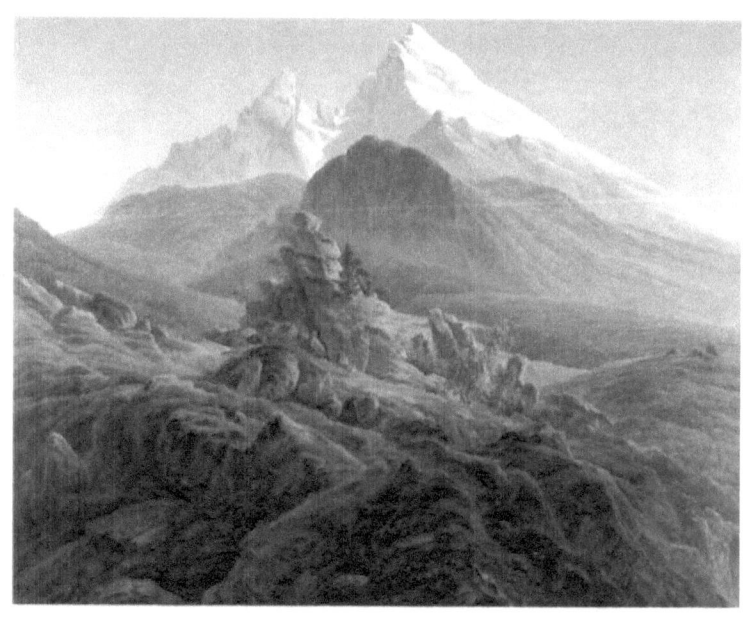

The Watzmann, 1824-1825, oil on canvas

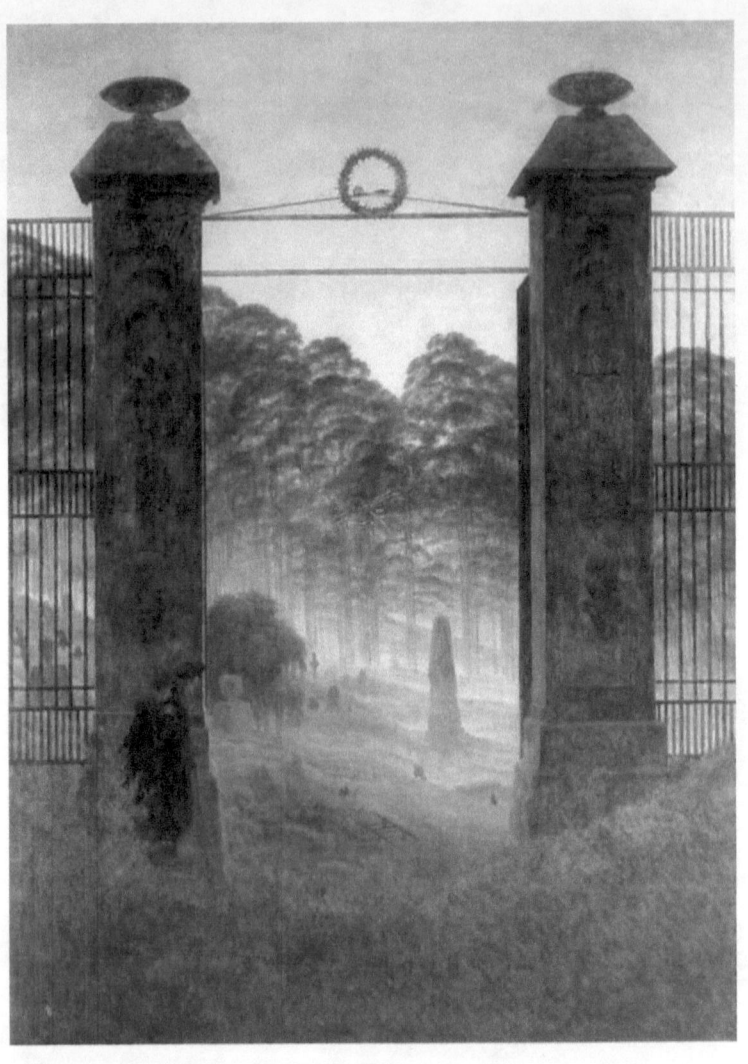

The Cemetery Entrance, 1825, oil on canvas

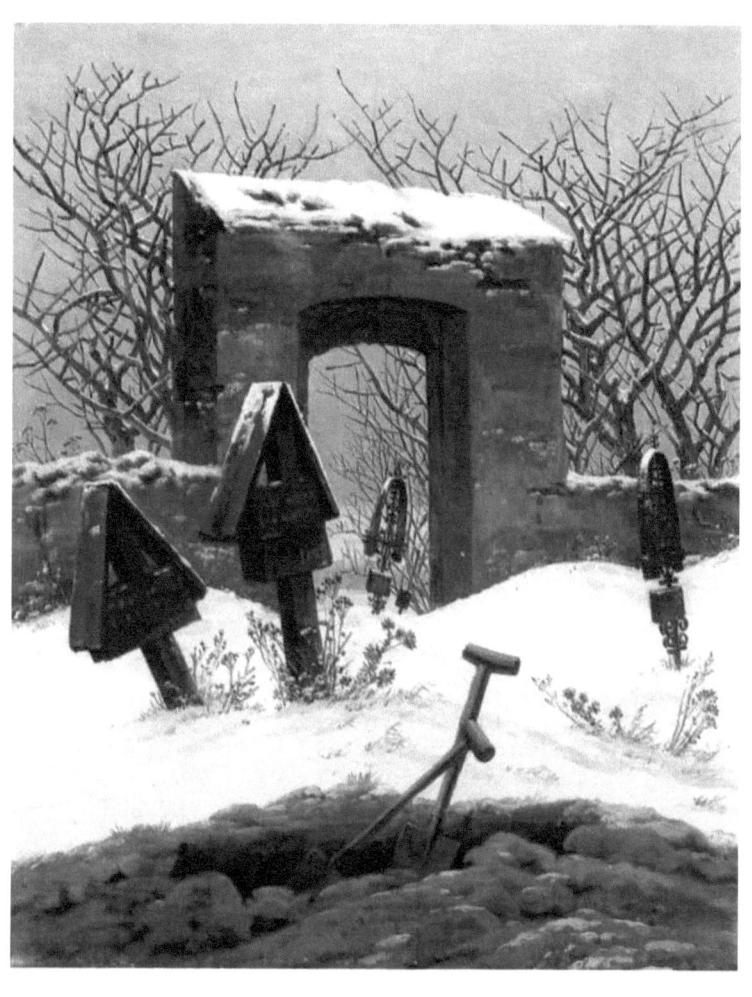

Graveyard under Snow, 1826, oil on canvas

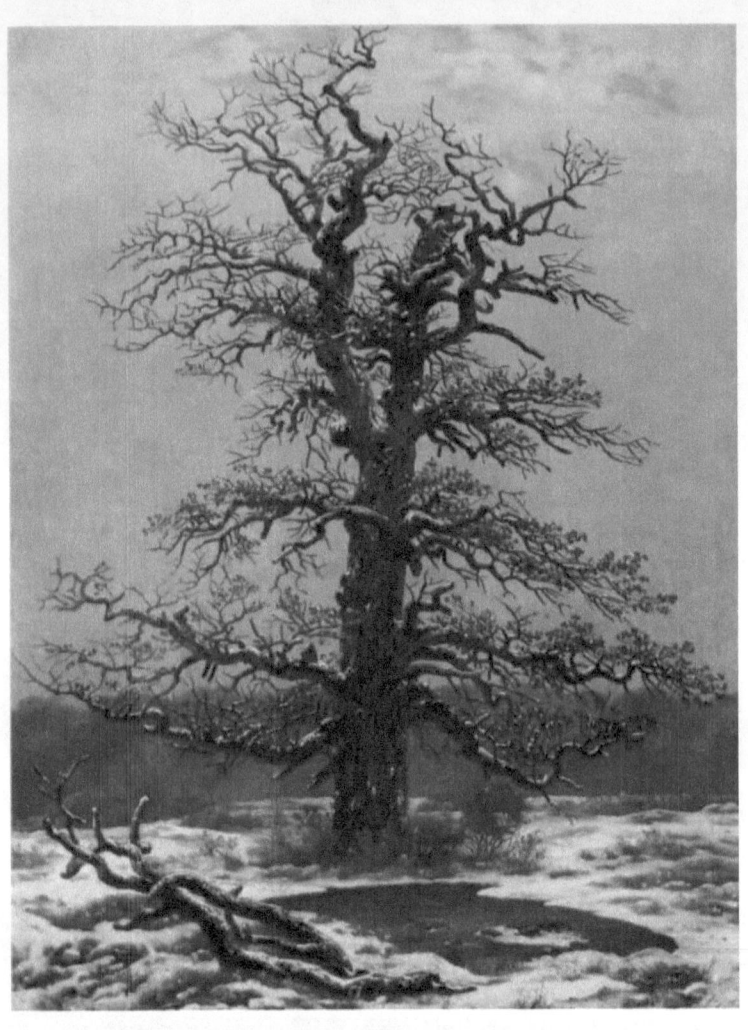

Oak tree in the snow, c.1827-c.1828, oil on canvas

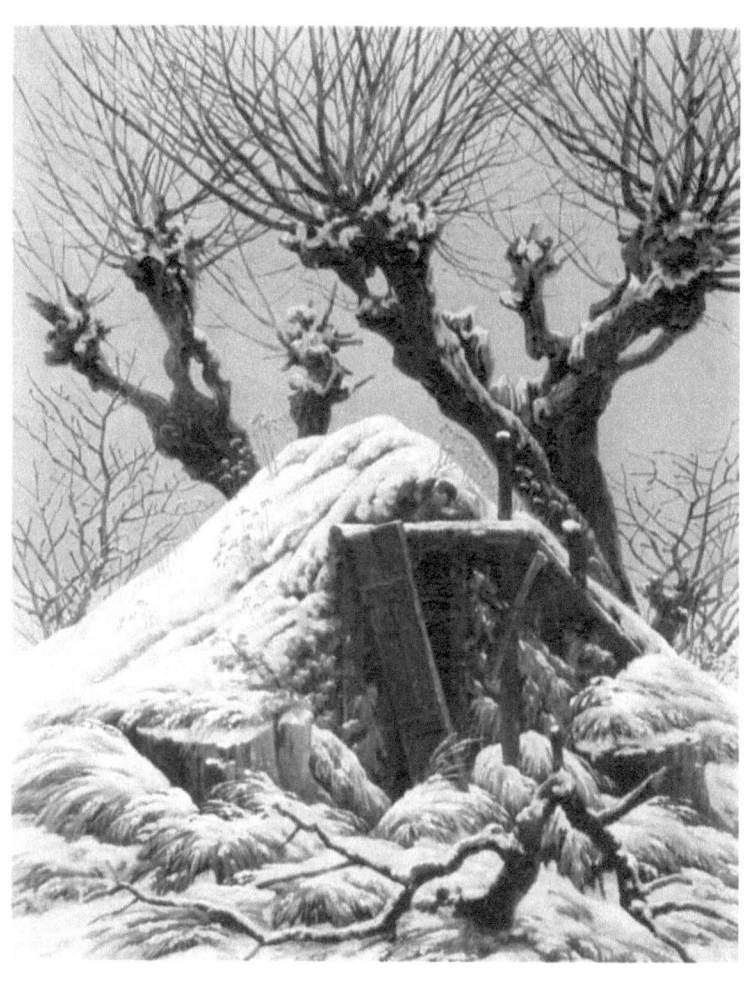

Trees in the snow, 1828, oil on canvas

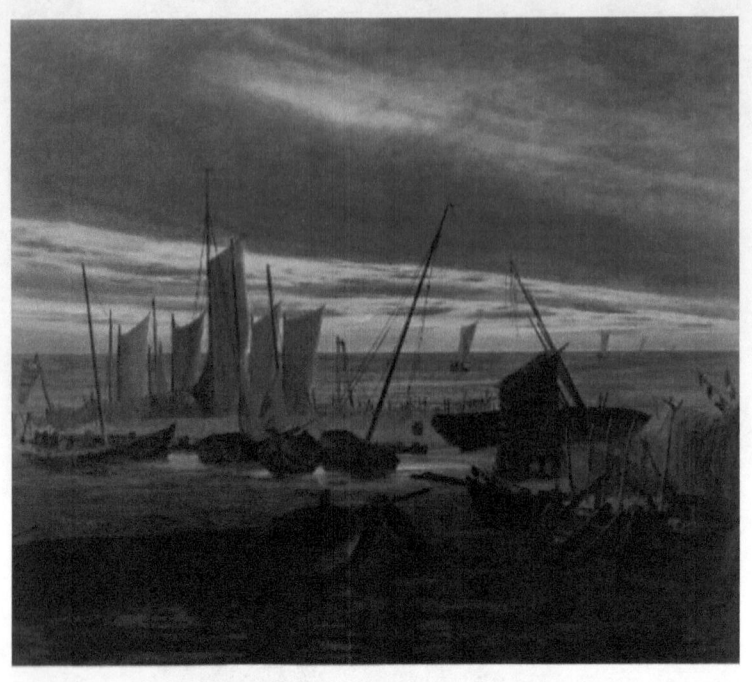

Boats in the Harbour at Evening, 1828, oil on canvas

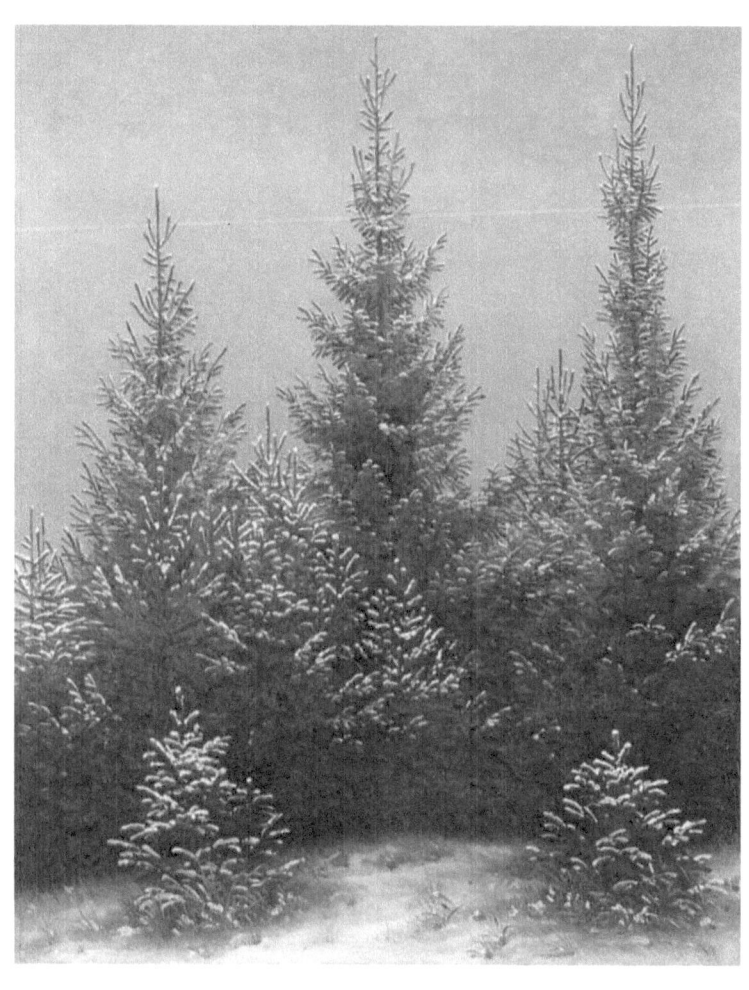

Fir Trees in the Snow, 1828, oil on canvas

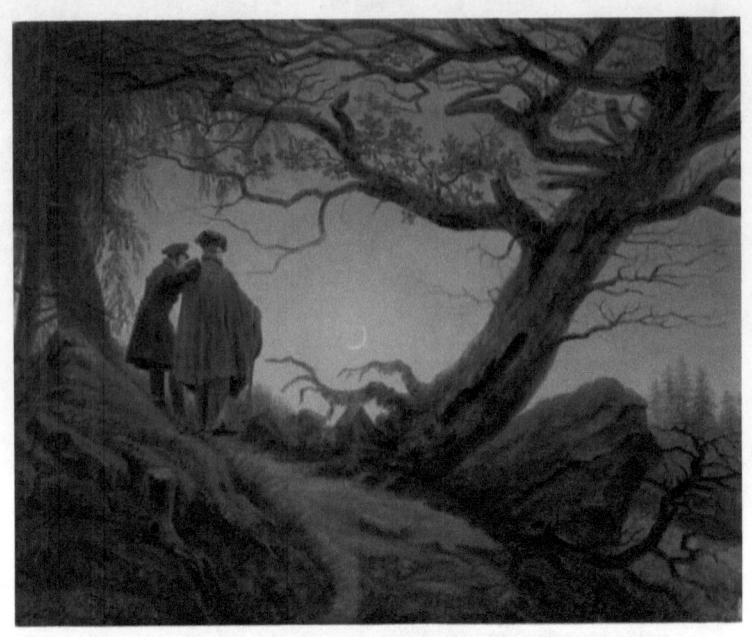

Two Men Contemplating the Moon, c.1825-c.1830, oil on canvas

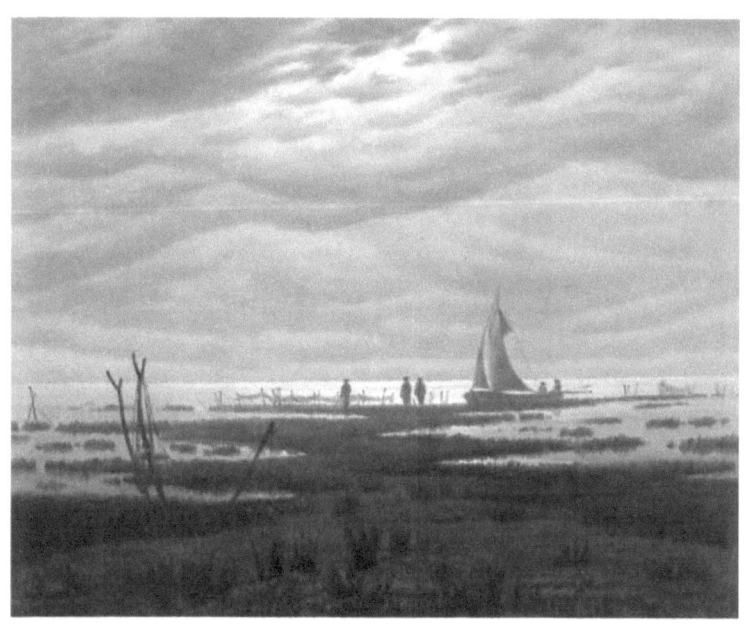

Flat country shank at Bay of Greifswald, 1834, oil on canvas

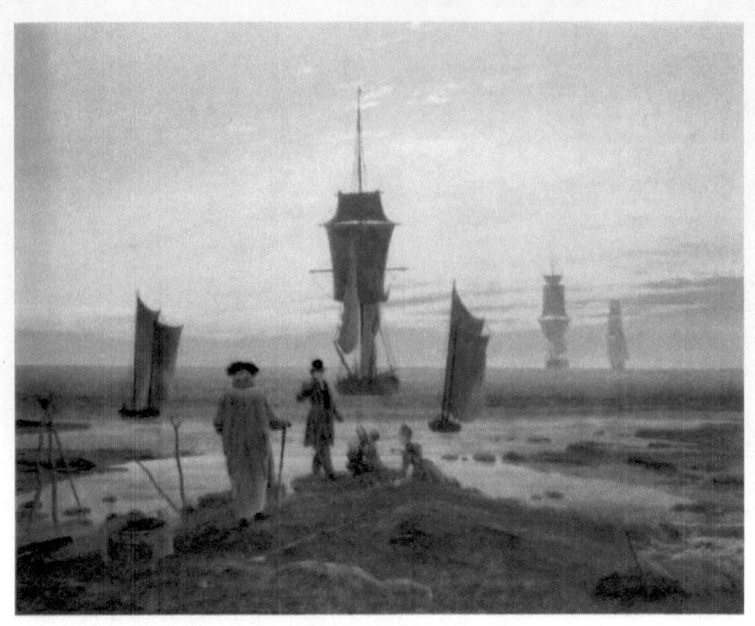

The stages of life, 1835, oil on canvas

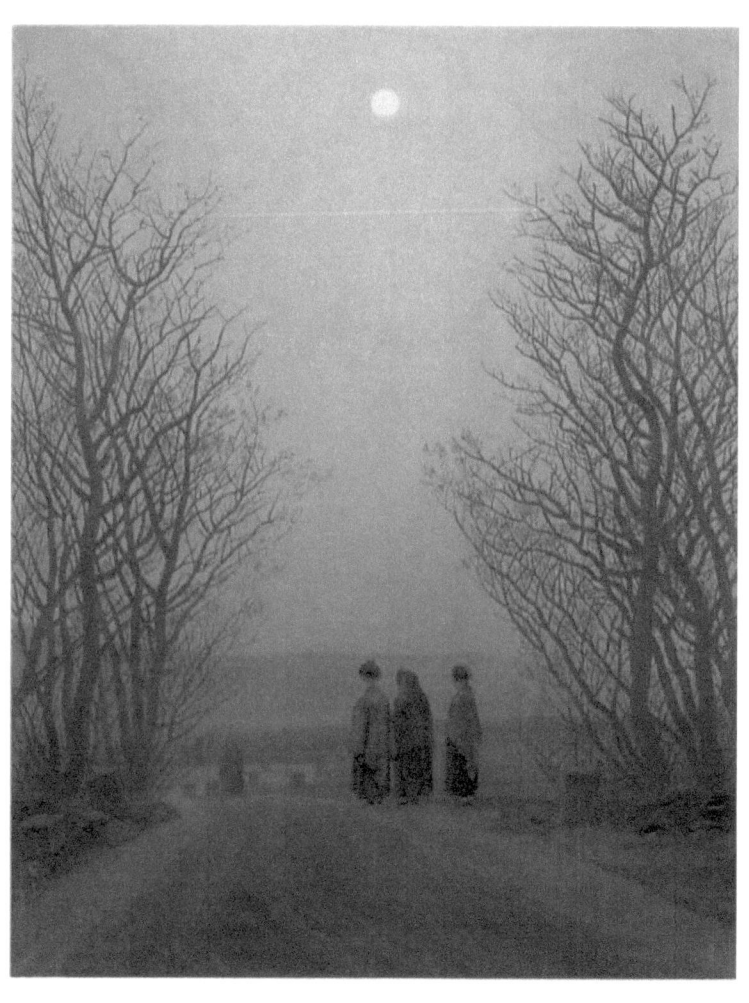

Easter Morning, 1835, oil on canvas

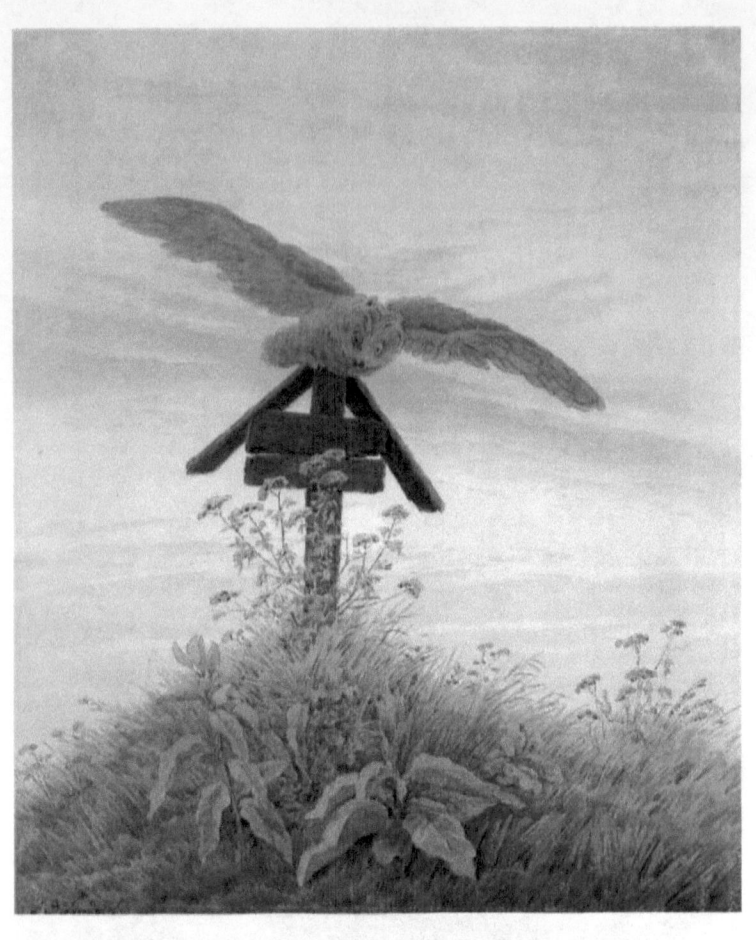

Owl on a grave, c.1836-c.1837, oil on canvas

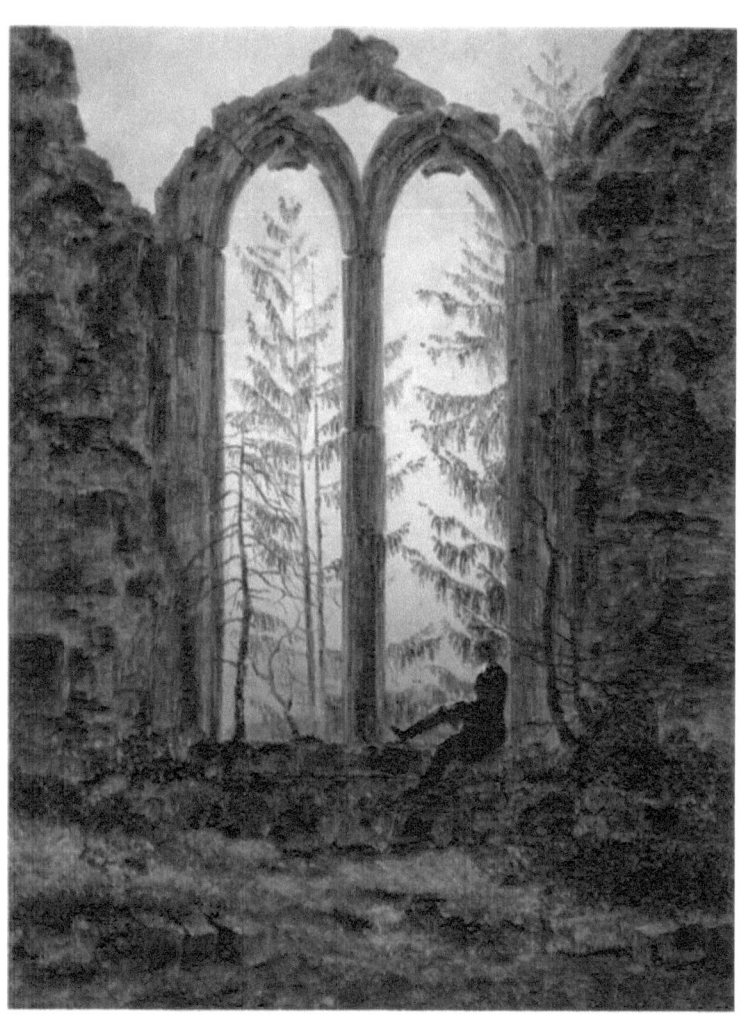

The dreamer, 1820-1840, oil on canvas

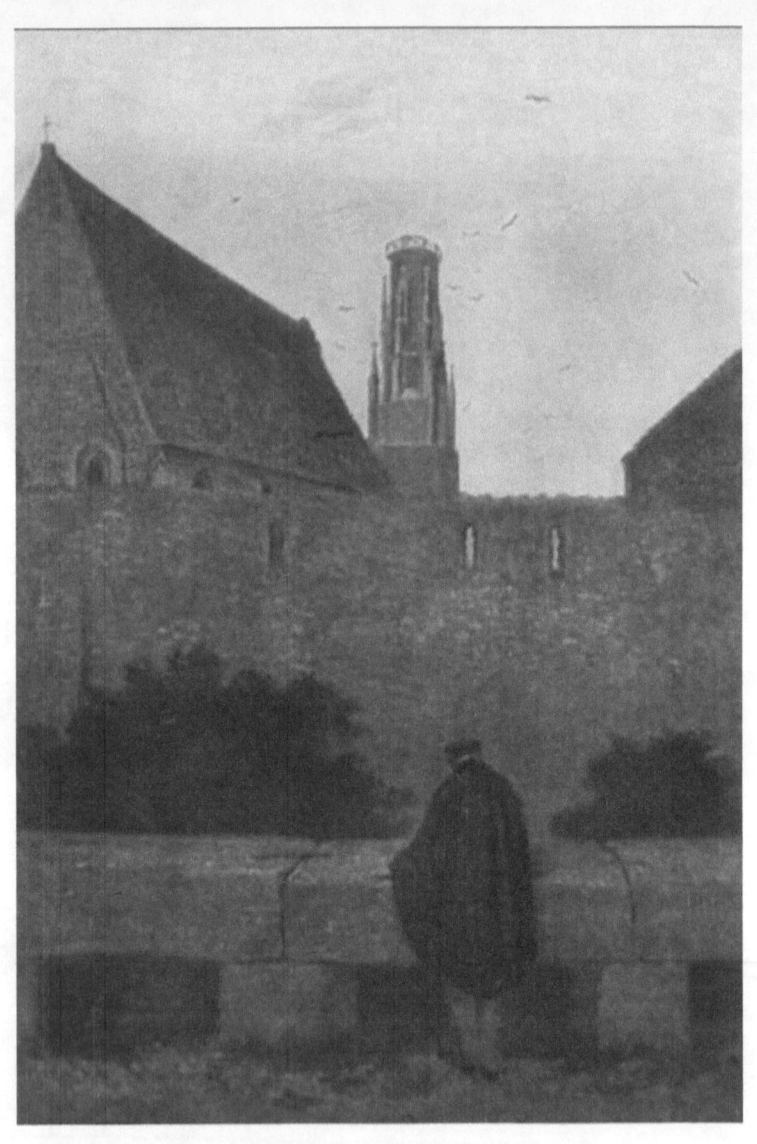

By the townwall, oil

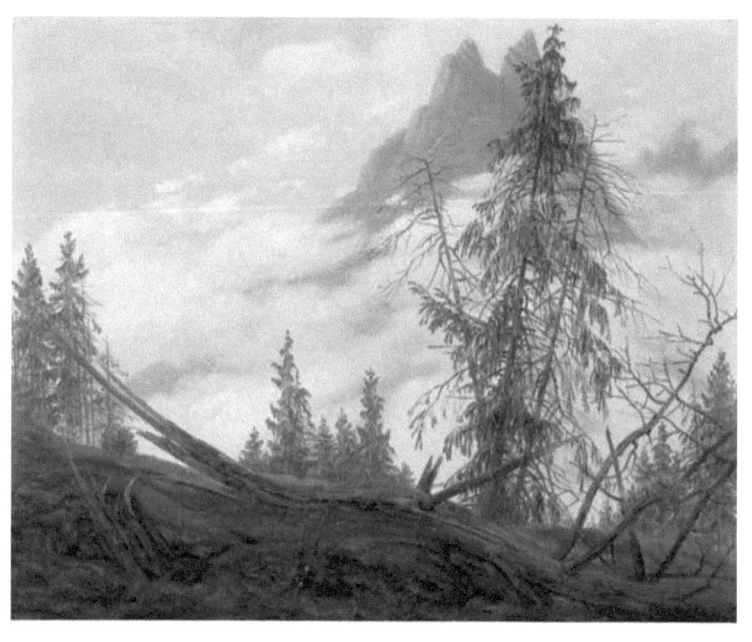

Mountain Peak with Drifting Clouds, oil

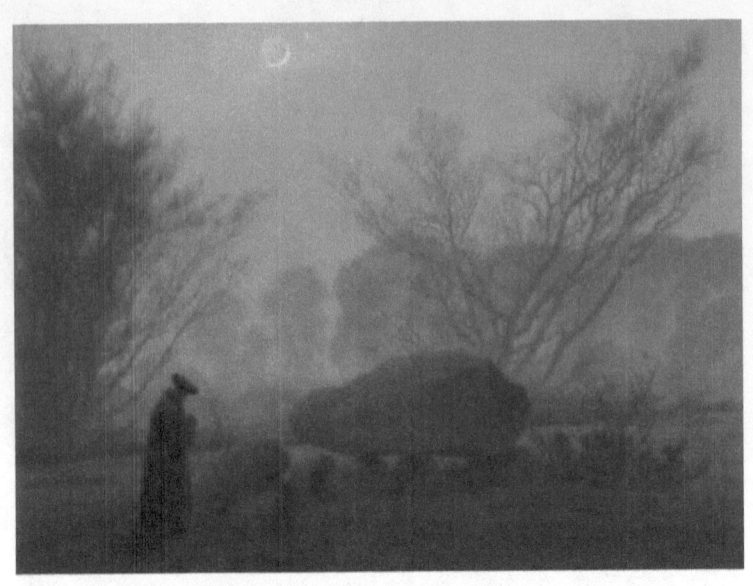

A Walk at Dusk, oil

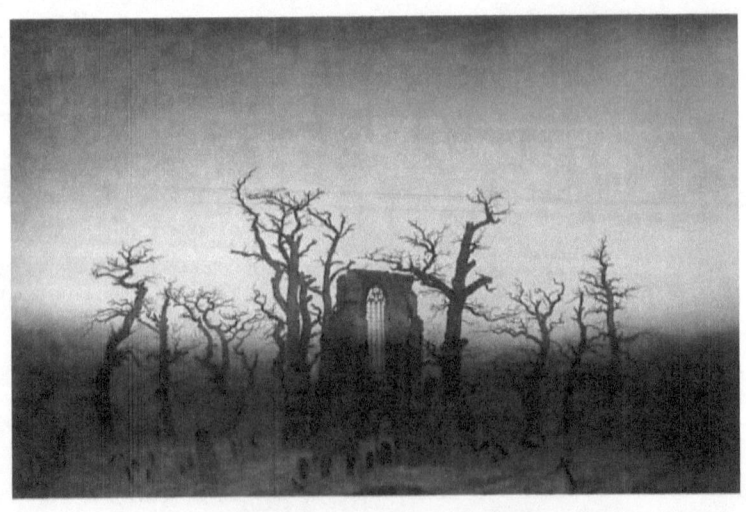

Abbey in Eichwald, oil

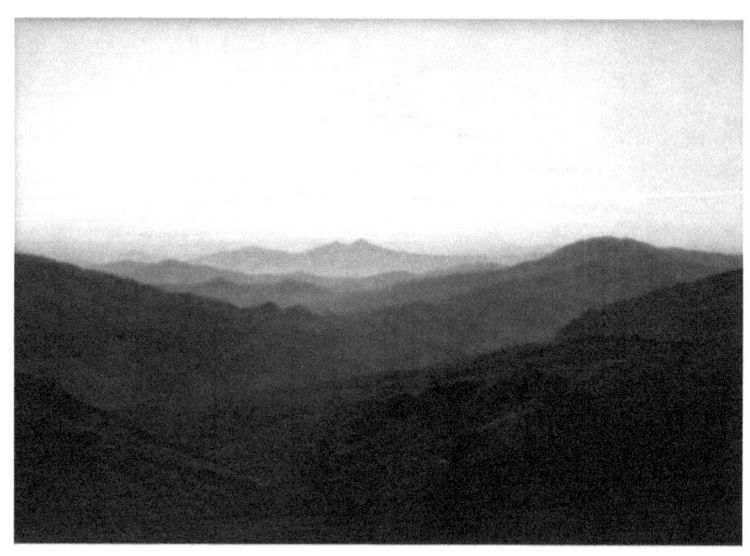

The Riesengbirge, oil

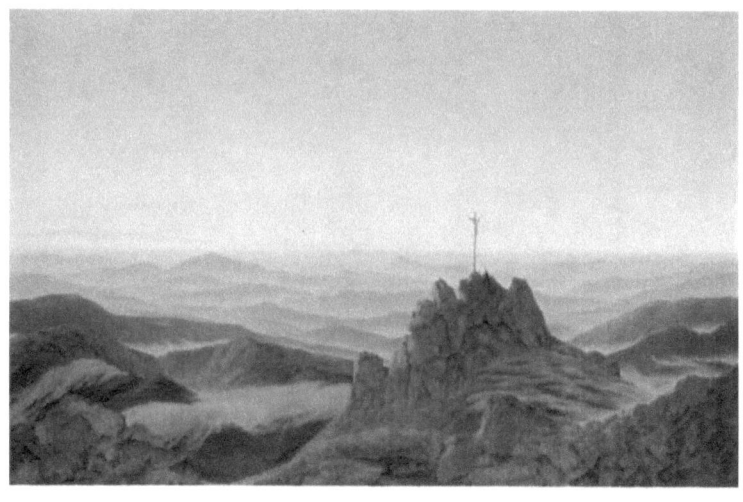

Morning in Riesengebirge, oil on canvas

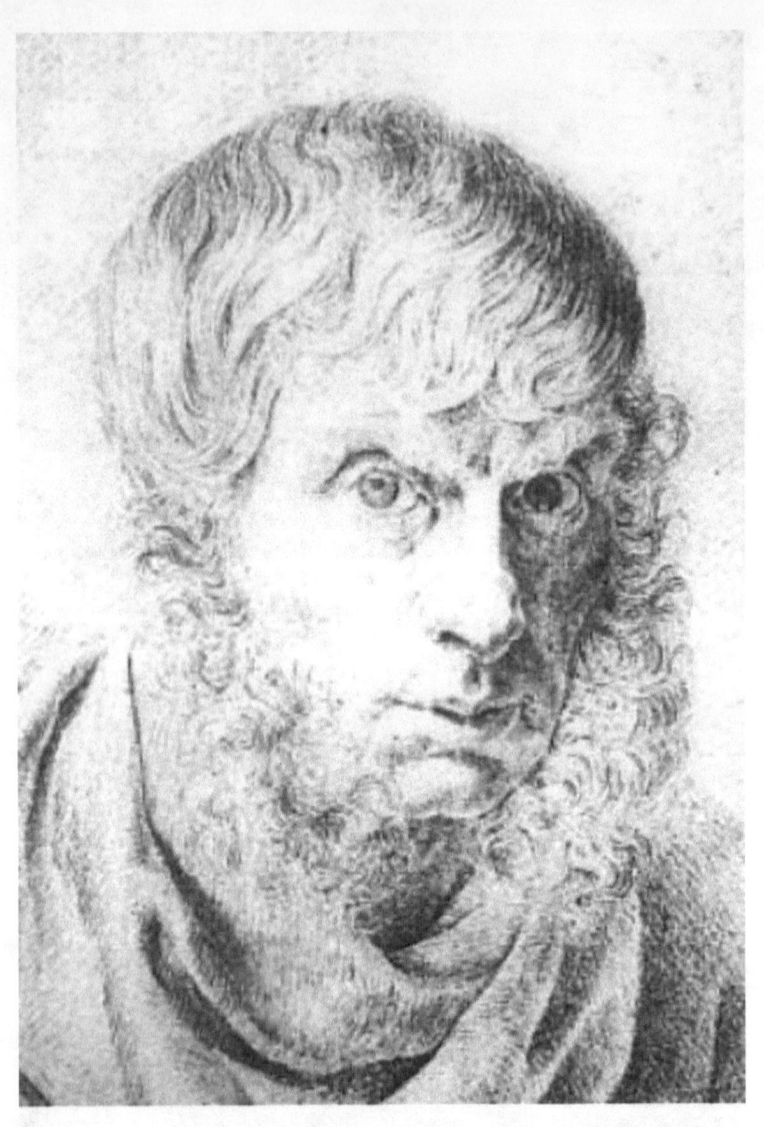

Self Portrait, drawing

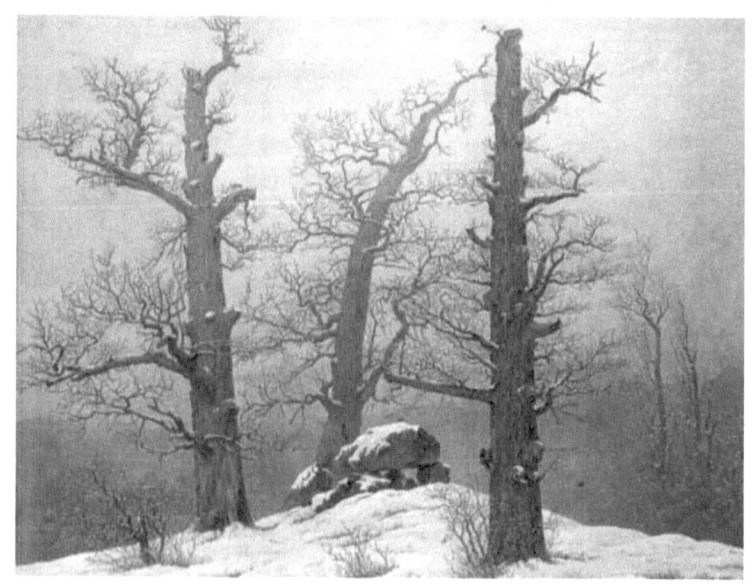

Winter Light, oil

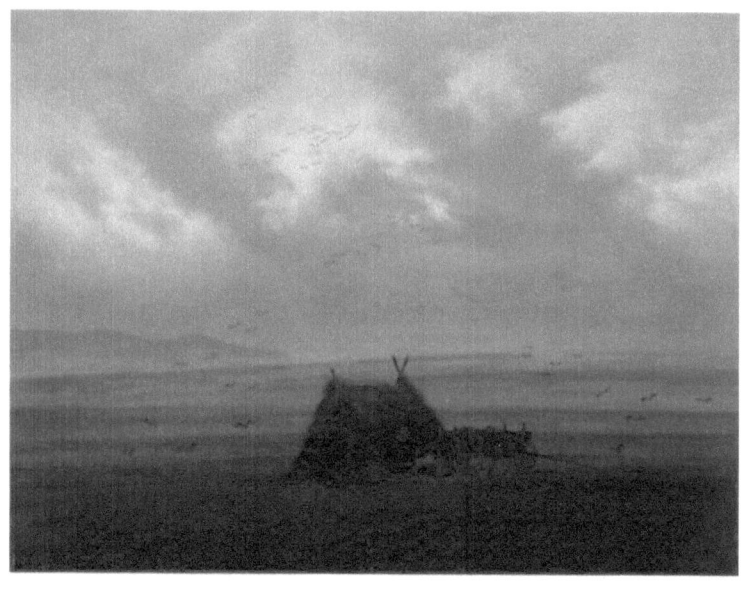

Fog, oil on canvas

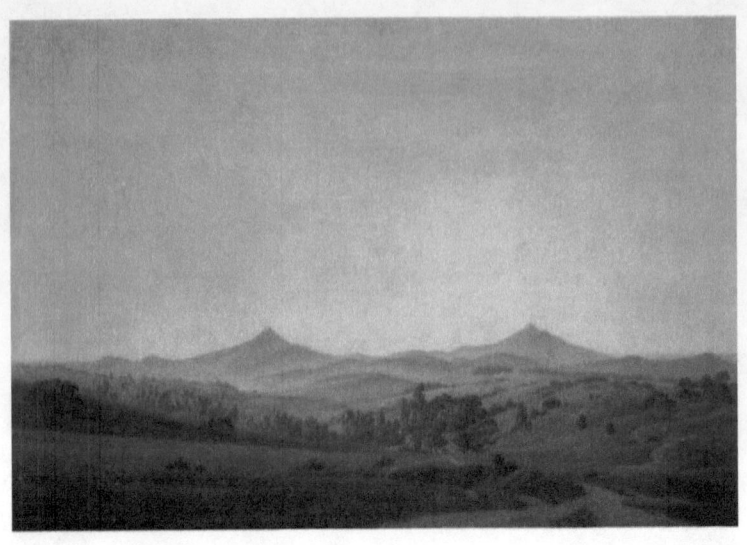

Bohemian Landscape with Mount Millsheauer, oil on canvas

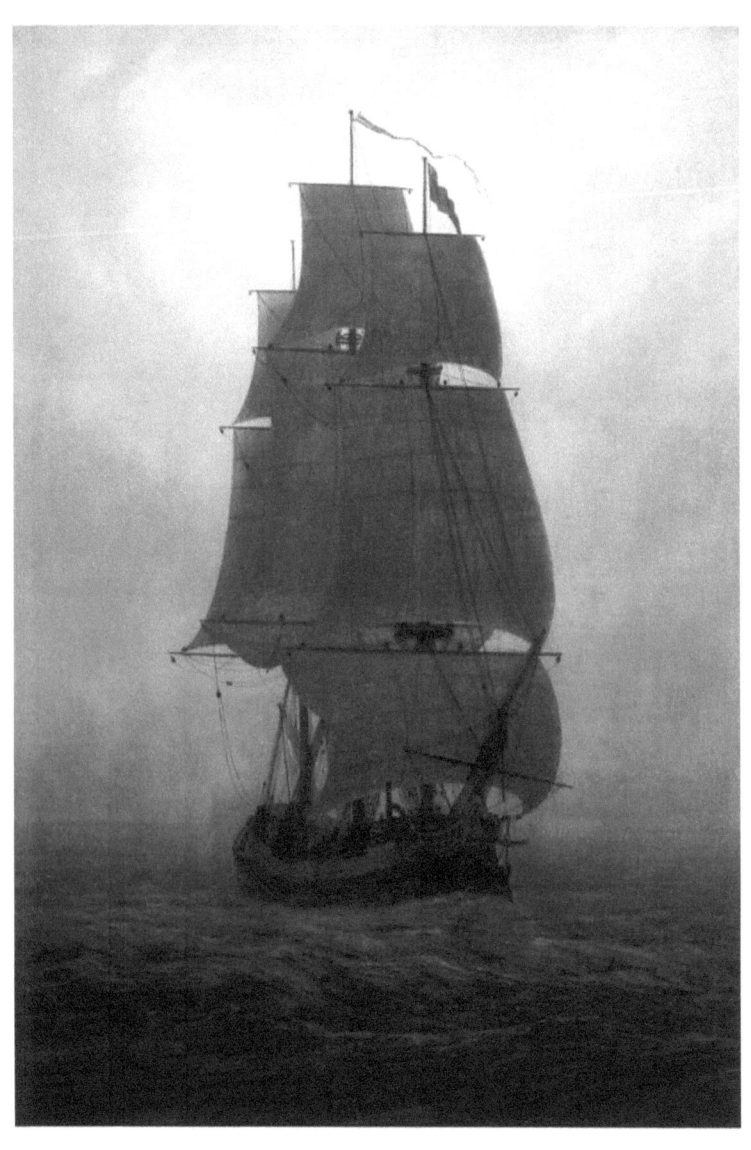

Sailing ship, oil on canvas

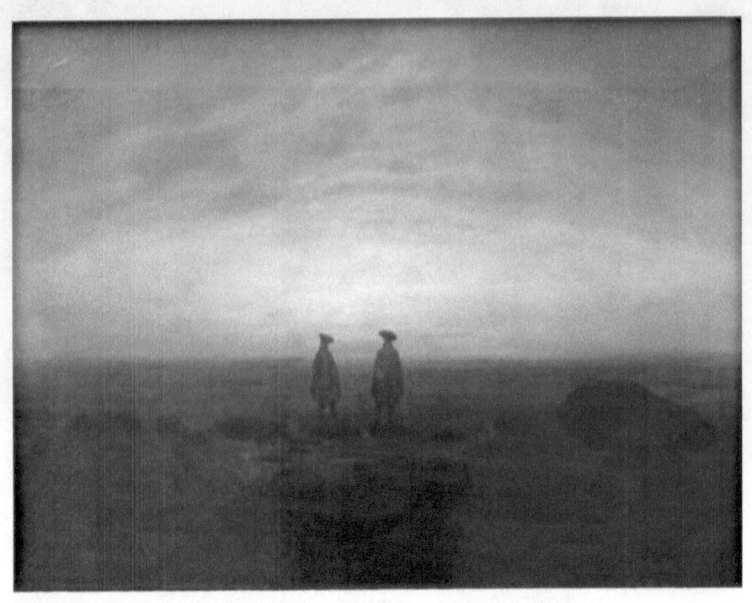

Two Men by the Sea, oil on canvas

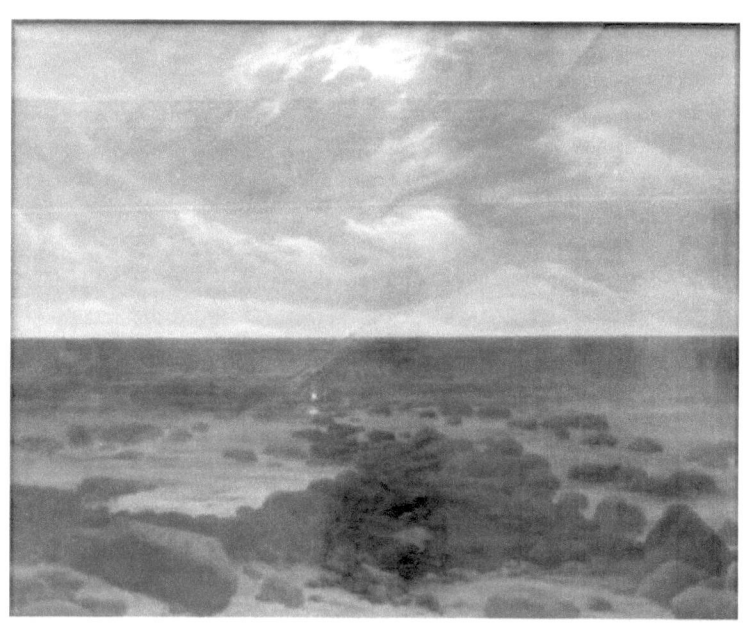

Coast Scene, oil on canvas

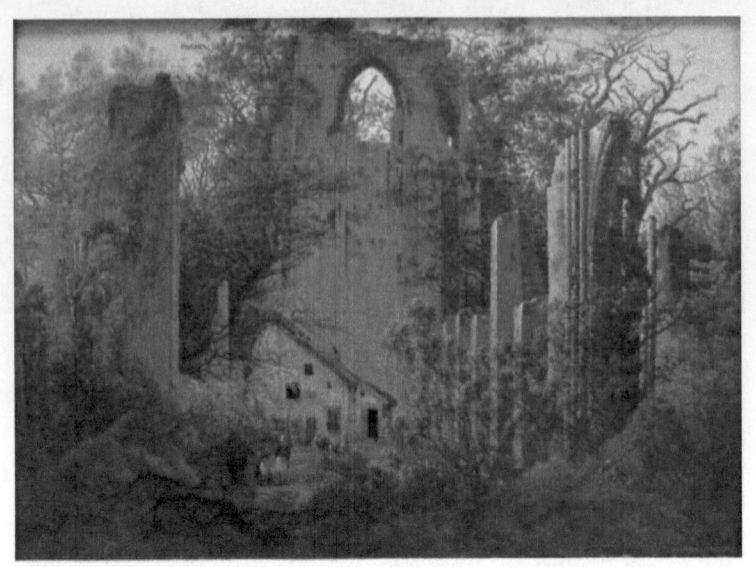

Eldena, oil

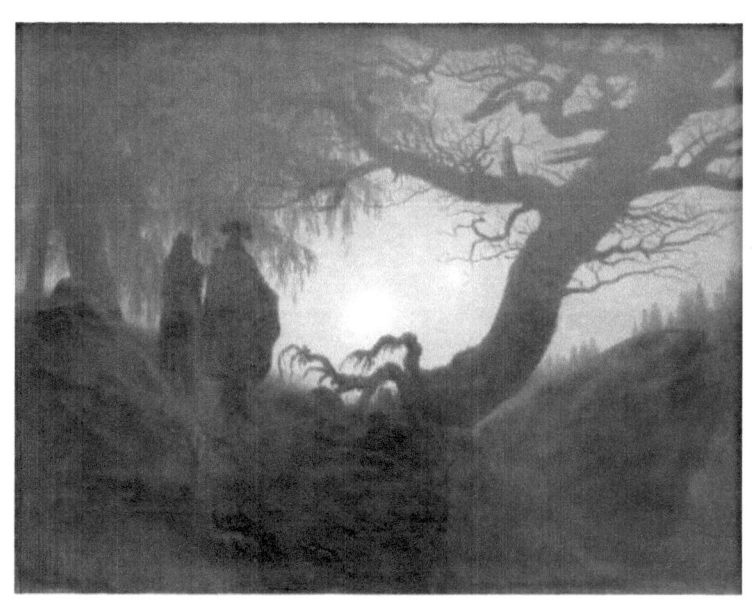

Man and Woman, oil

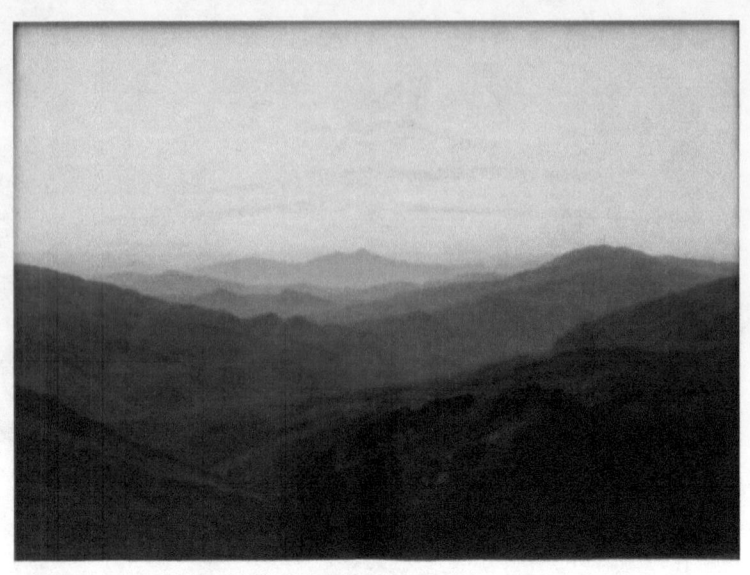

Riesengebirge, oil on canvas

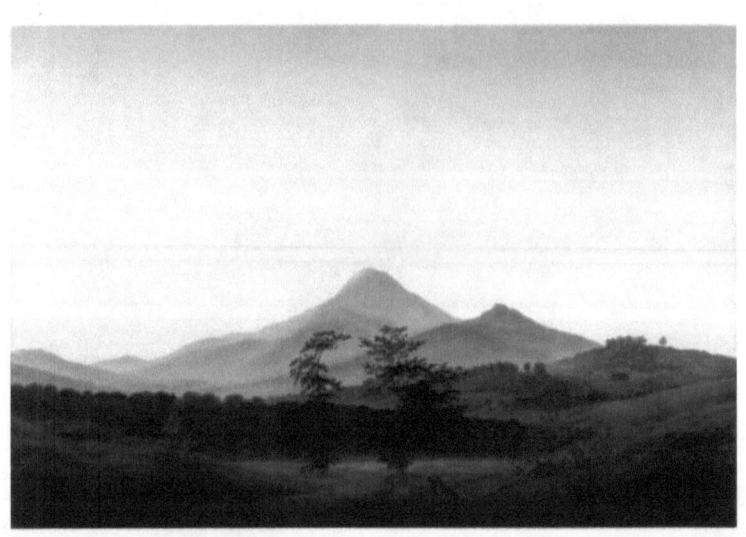

Bohemian Landscape, oil on canvas

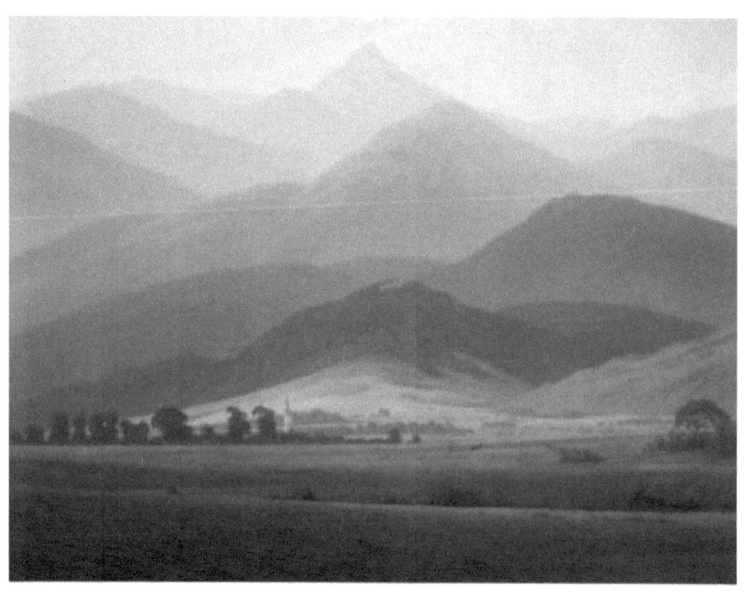

View from the Small Warmbrunn Sturmhaube, oil on canvas

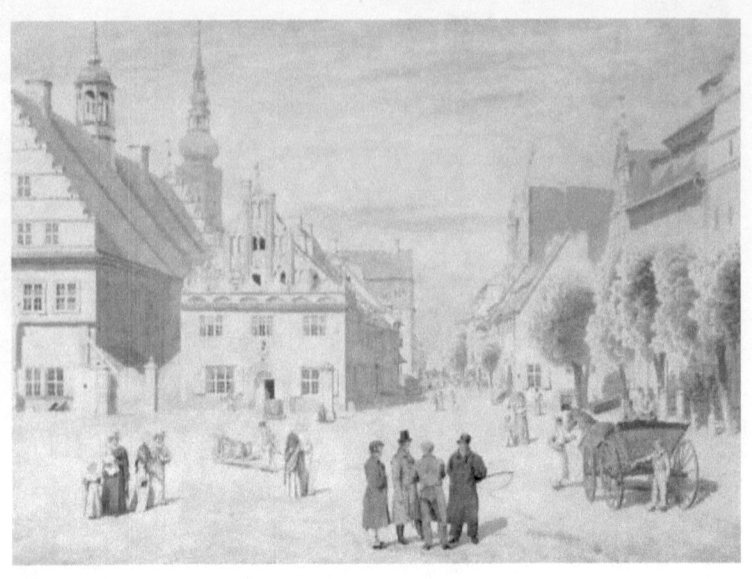

Greifswald market, watercolor

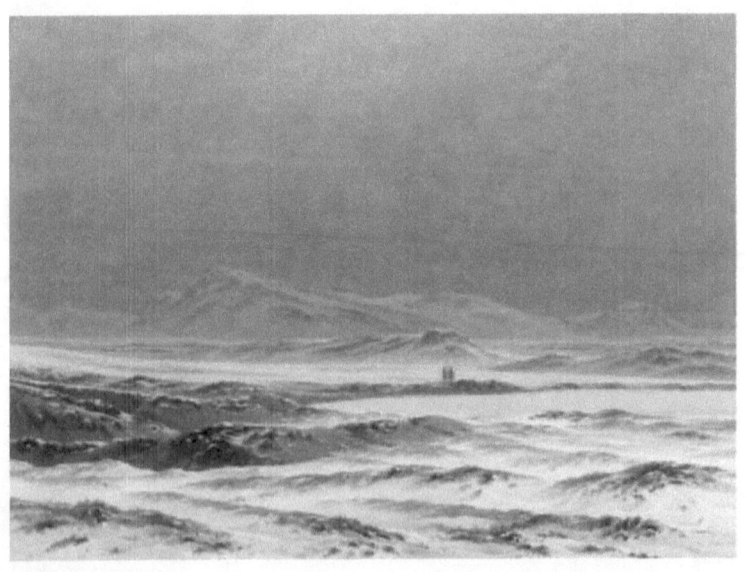

A Northern Spring Landscape, oil on canvas

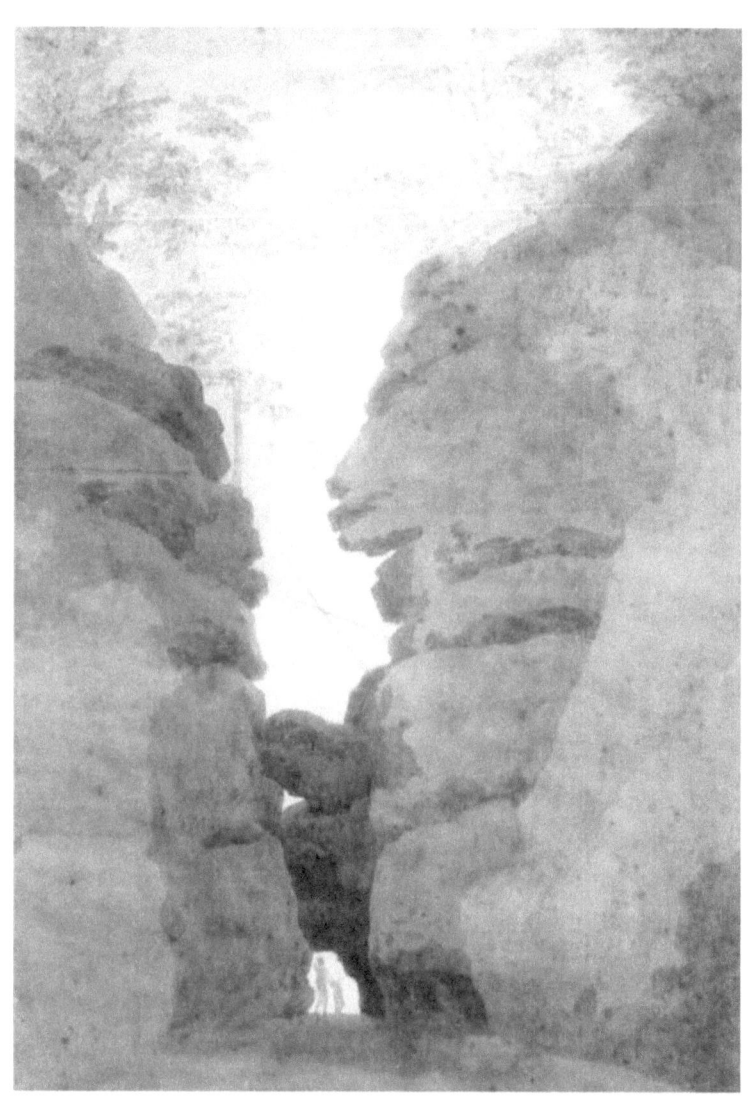

Rock arch in the Uttewalder Grund

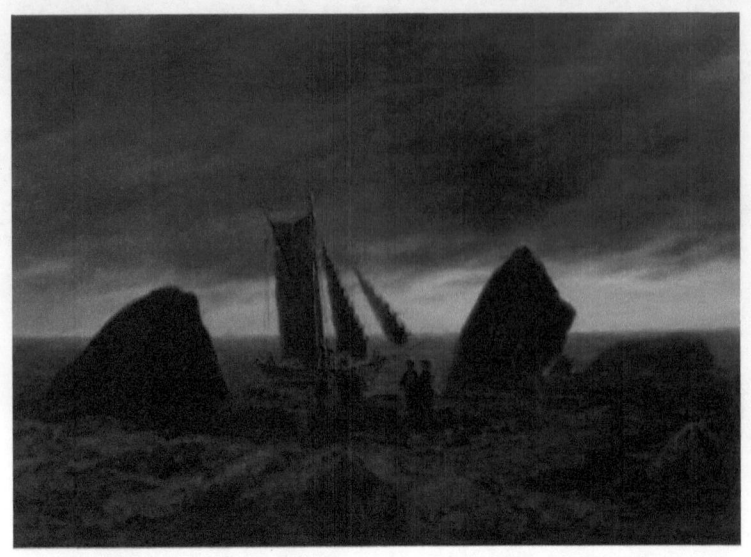

Fishing boat between two rocks on the beach of the
Baltic Sea, oil

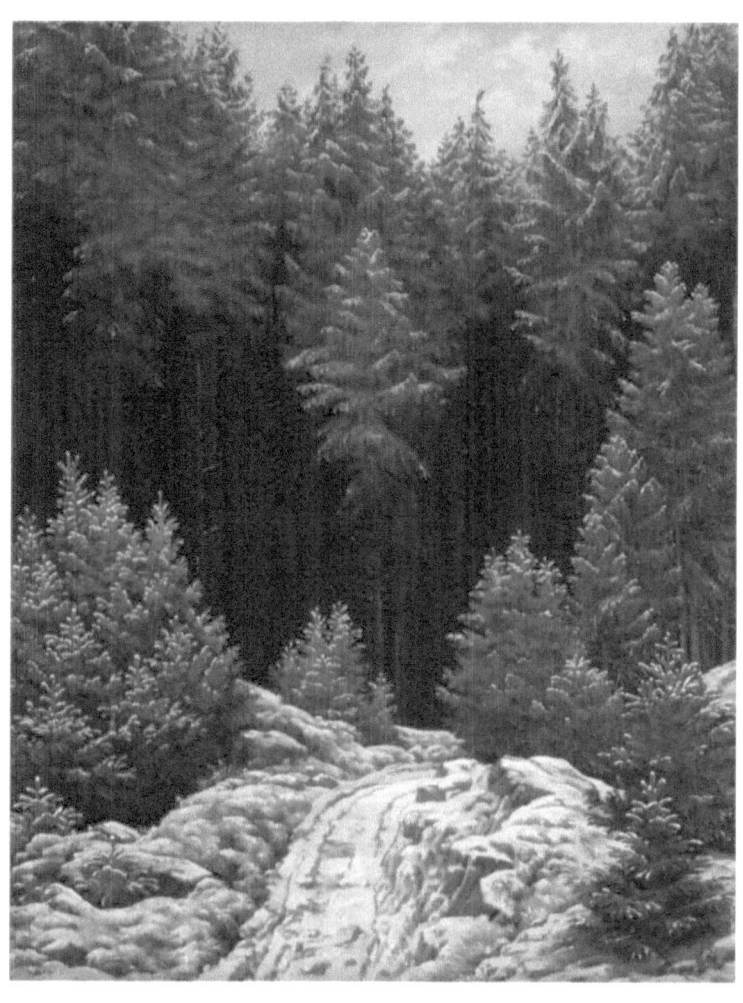

Early snow, oil on canvas

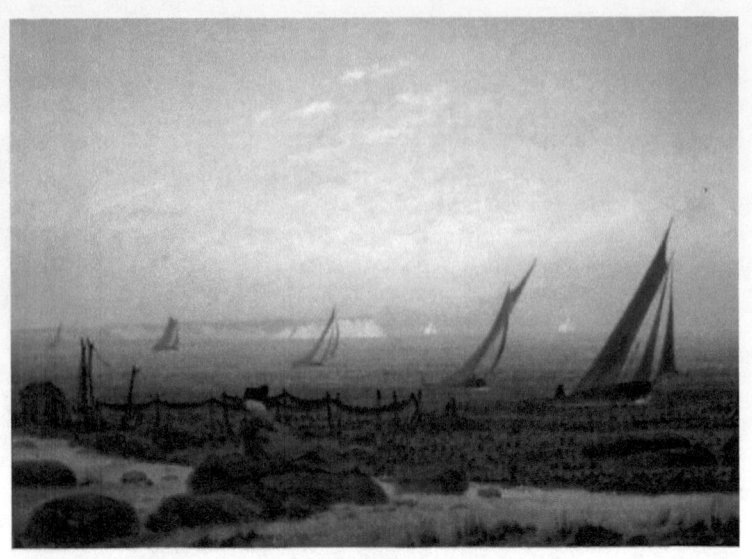

Woman on the beach of Ruegen

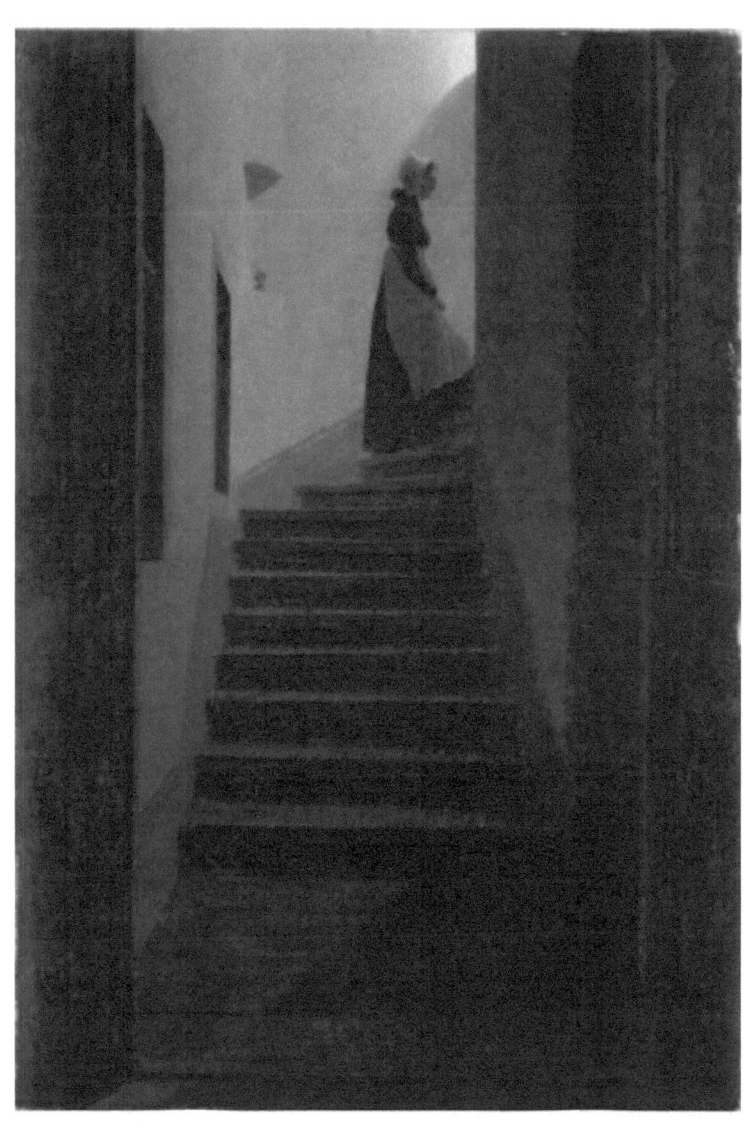

Woman on the stairs, oil

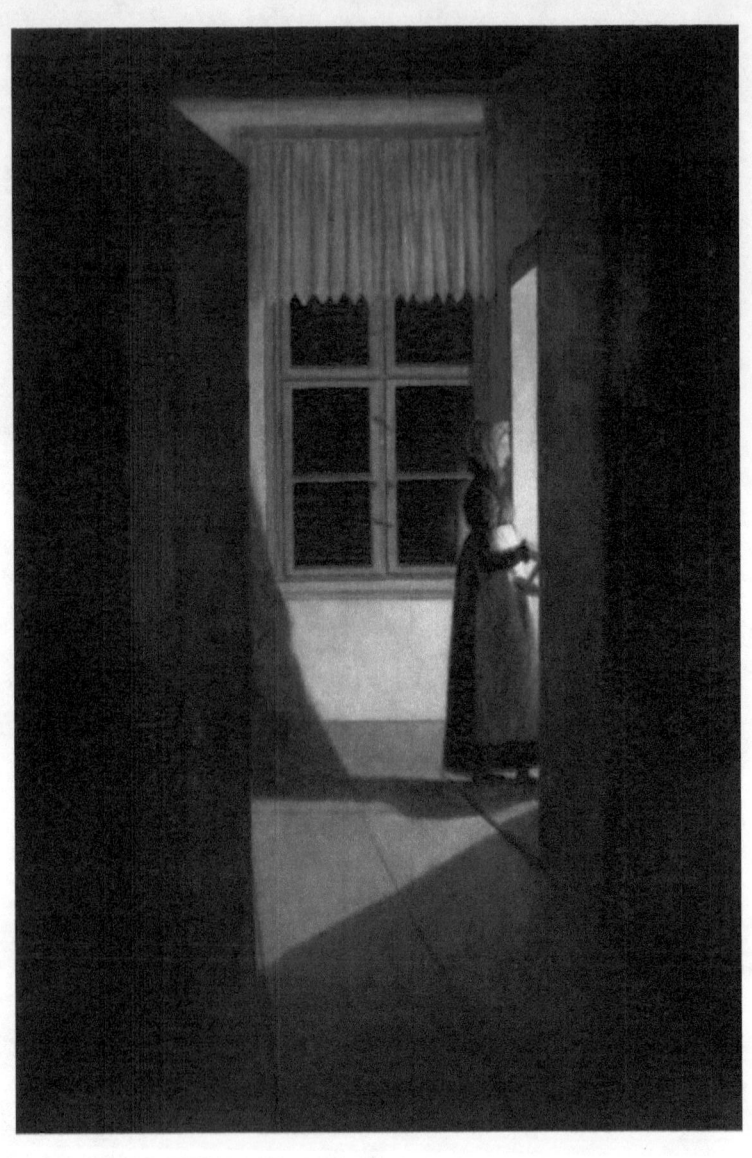

Woman with a candlestick, oil

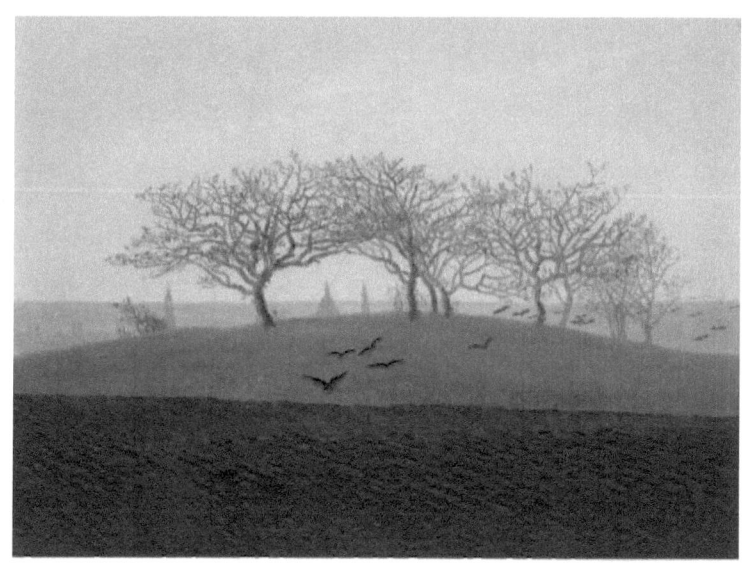

Hills and Ploughed Fields near Dresden, oil

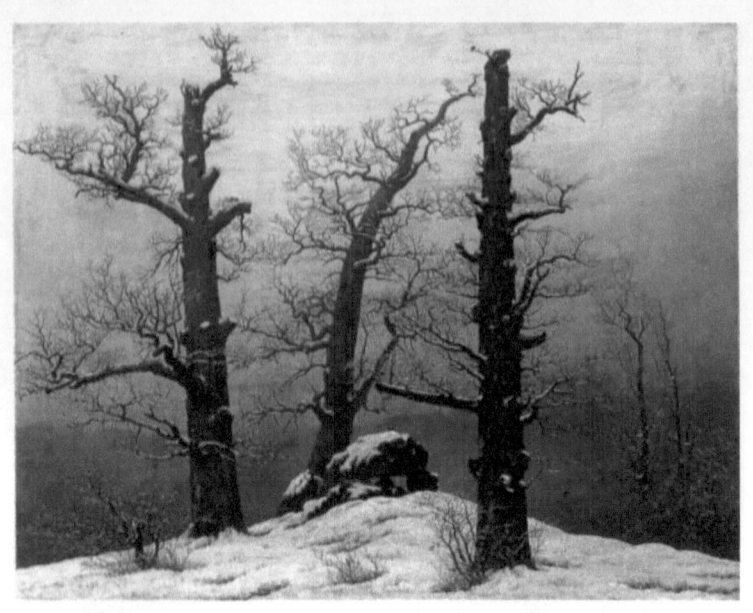

Passage grave in the snow, oil on canvas

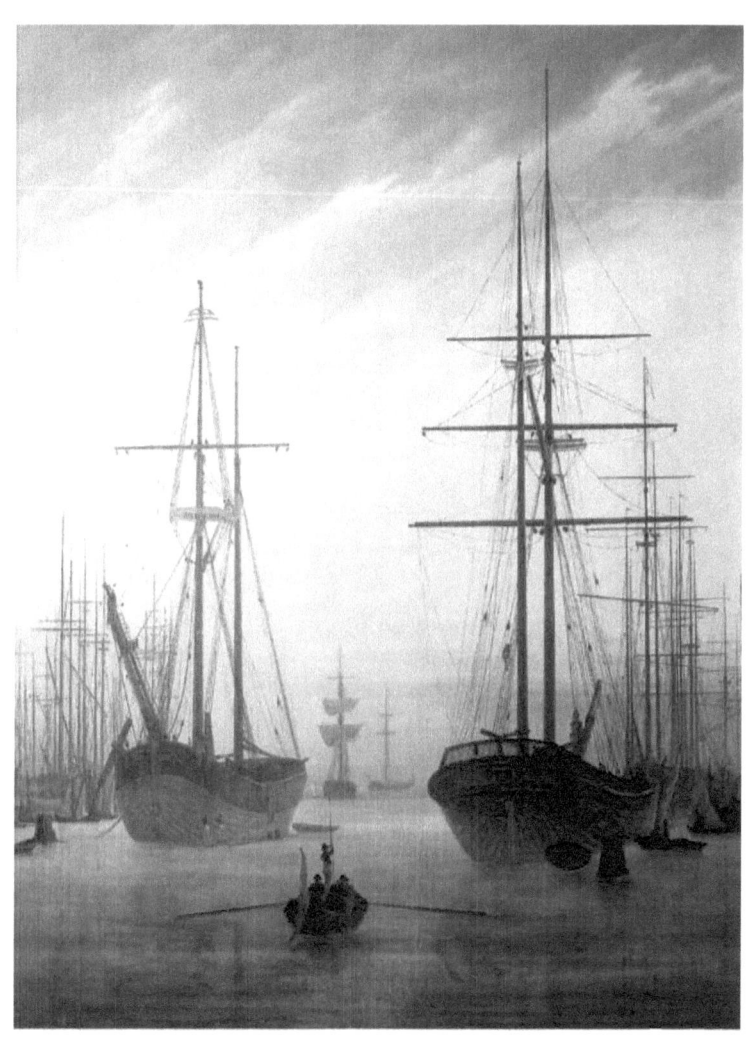

View of a harbour, oil on canvas

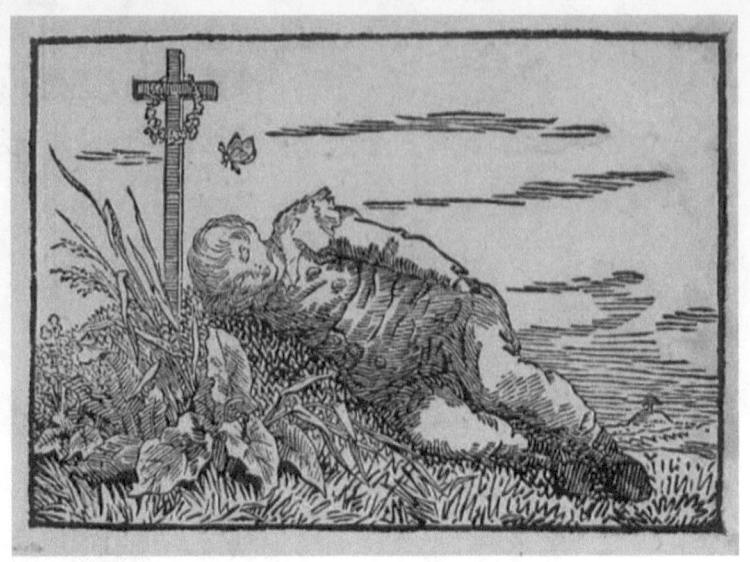

Boy sleeping on a grave, engraving

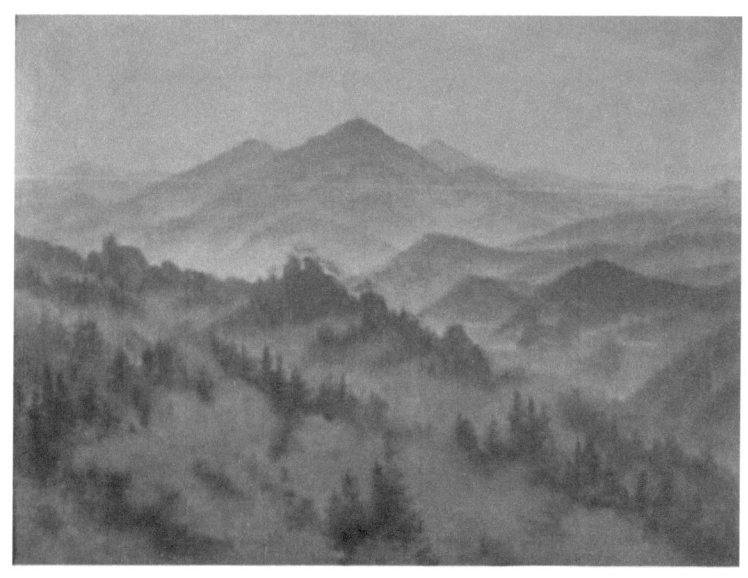

Landscape with the Rosenberg in Bohemian
Switzerland

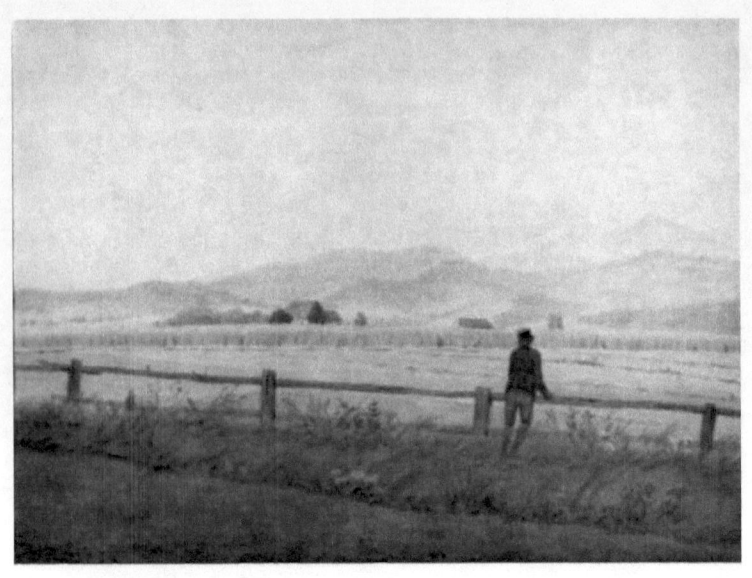

Landscape with a male figure

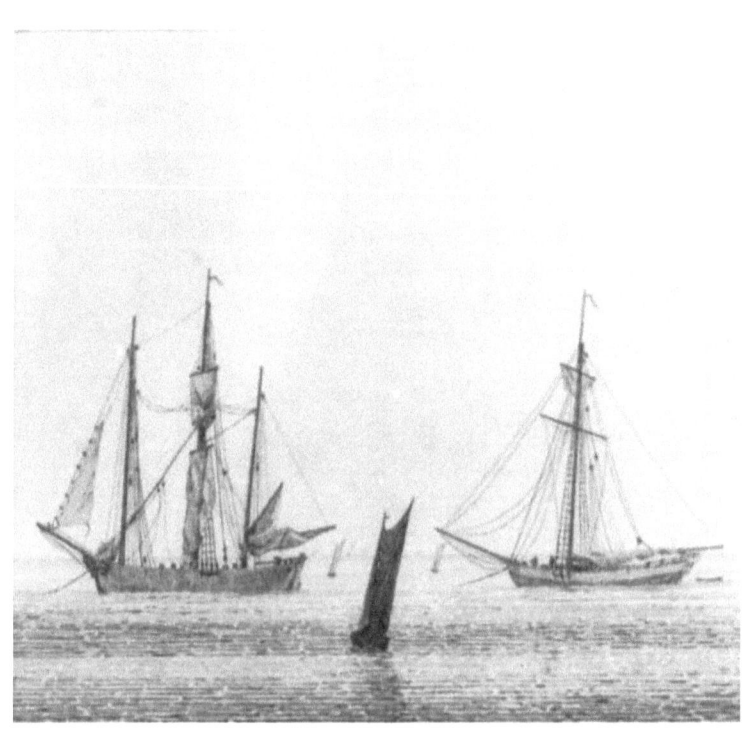

Sea with ships, engraving

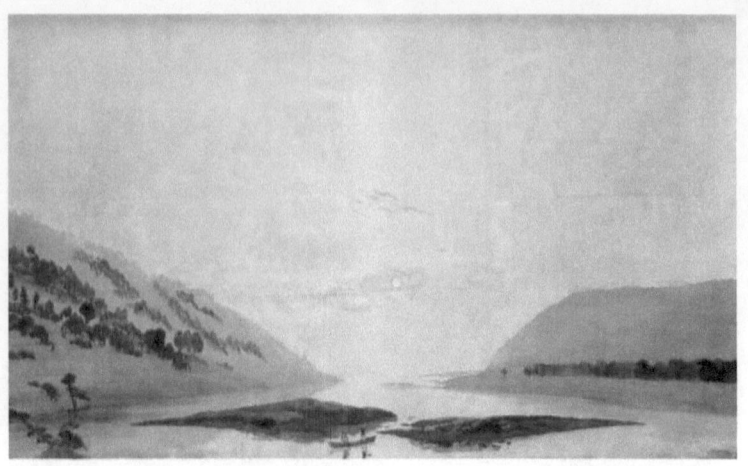

Mountainous River Landscape

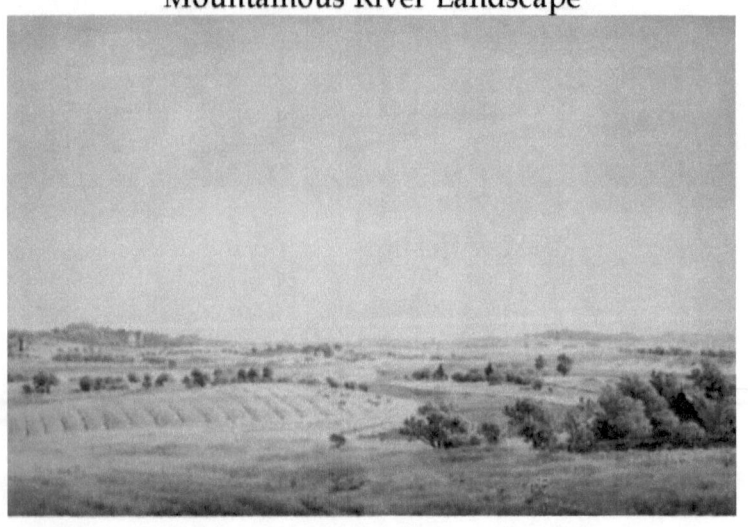

Rogen landscape in Putbus

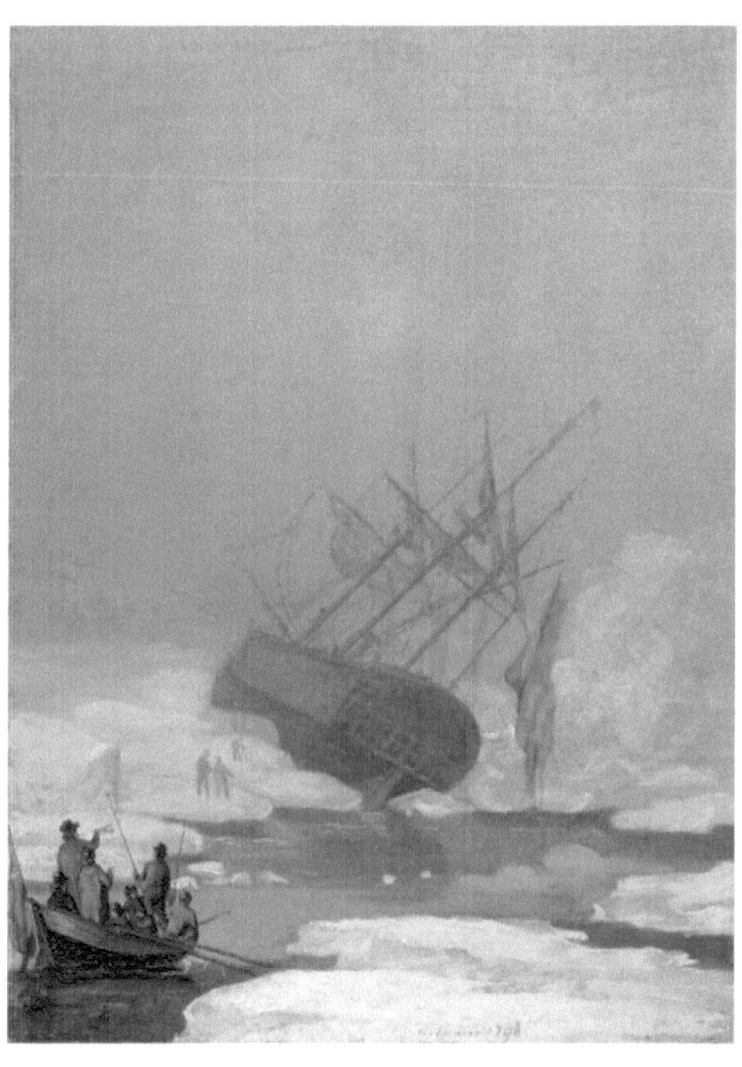

Ship in the Arctic Ocean, oil on canvas

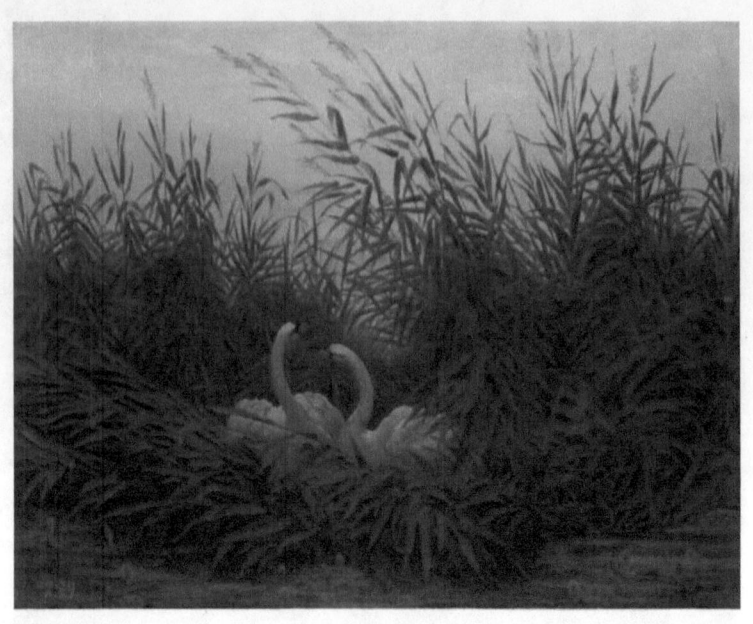

Swans among the reeds at the first Morgenro, oil

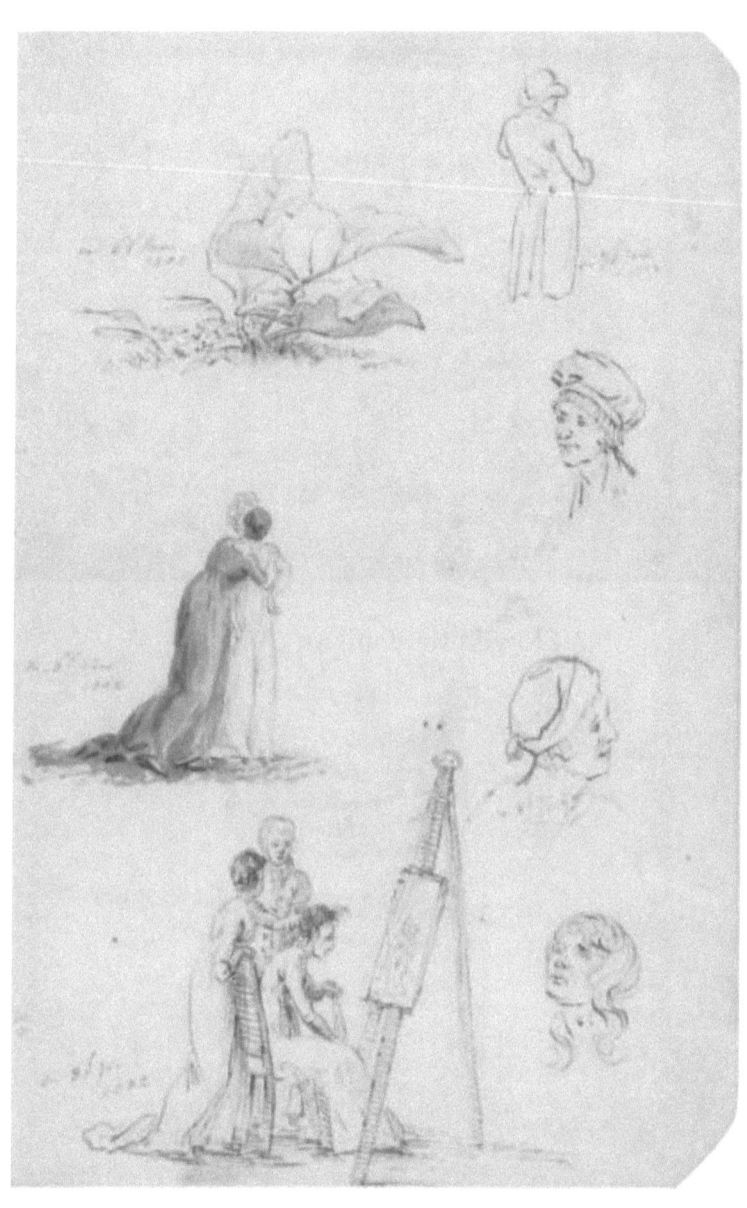

Study of heads, figures, and foliage

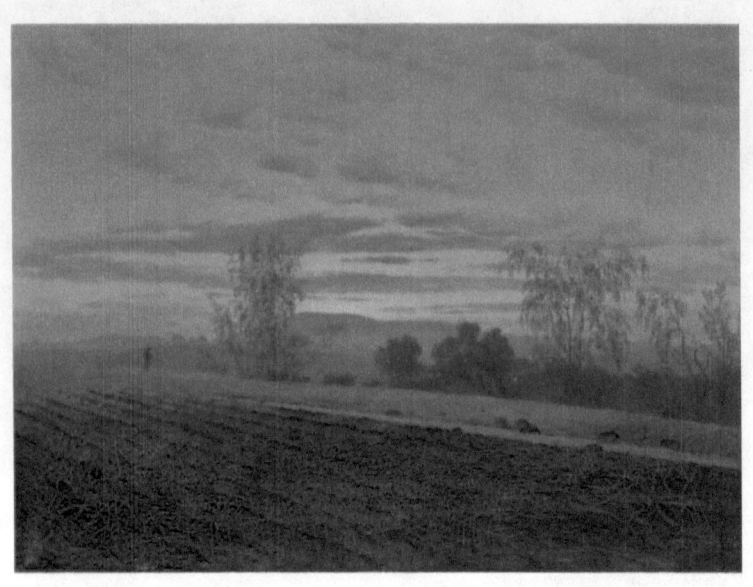

Plowed field, oil on canvas

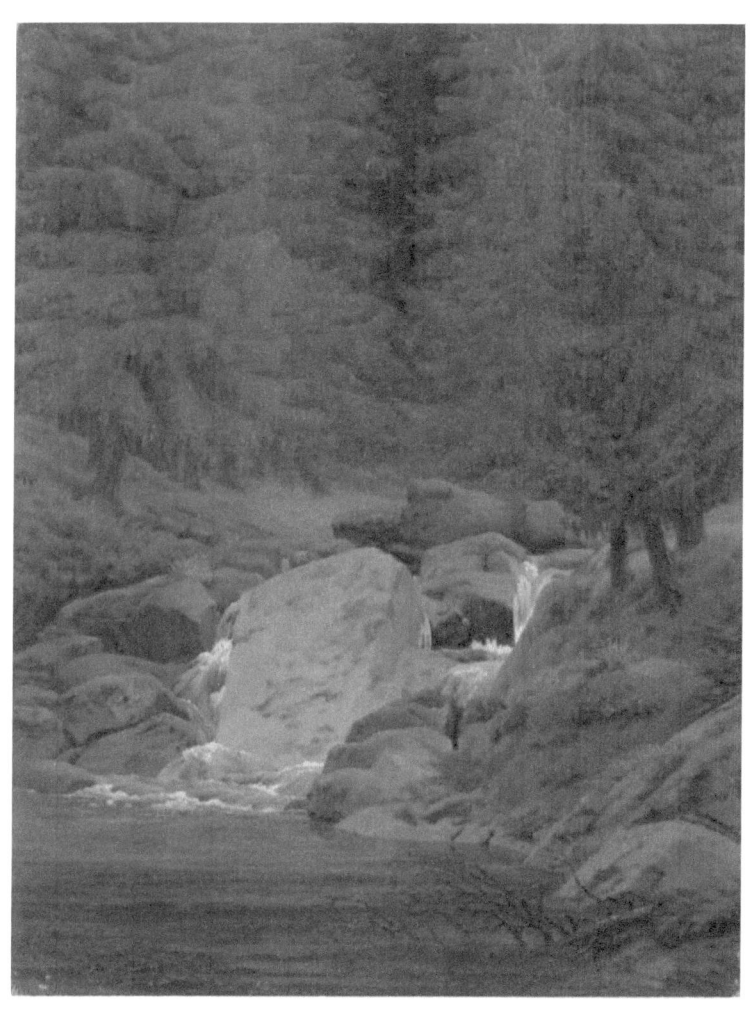

Pines at the waterfall, oil on canvas

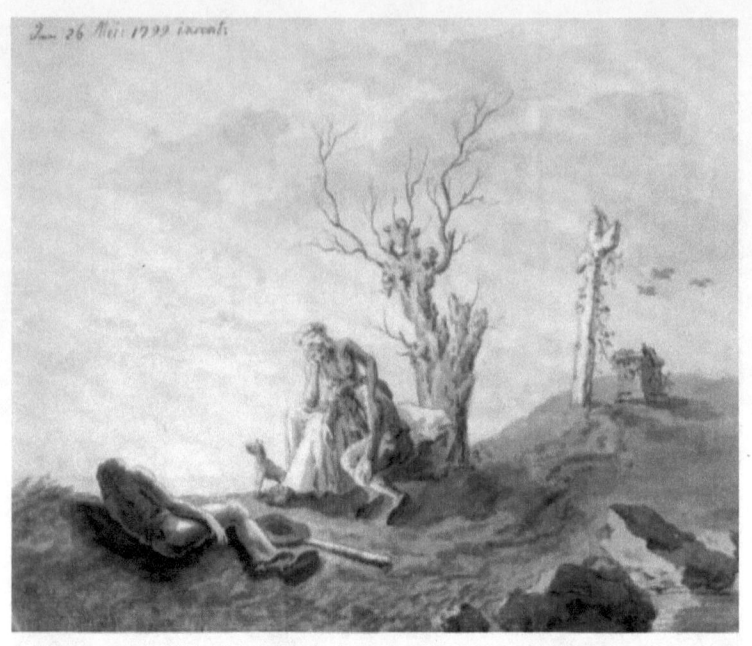

Funeral scene at the beach, drawing

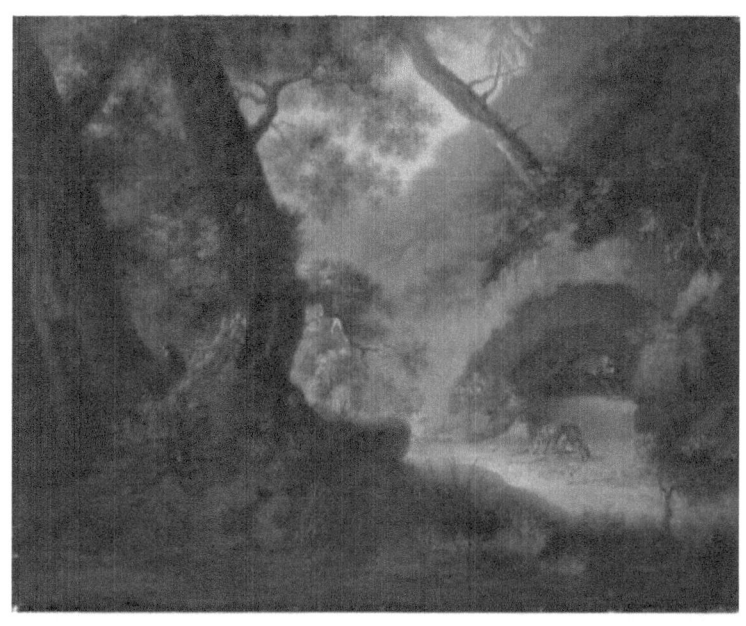

Wolves in the forrest in front of a cave, oil on canvas

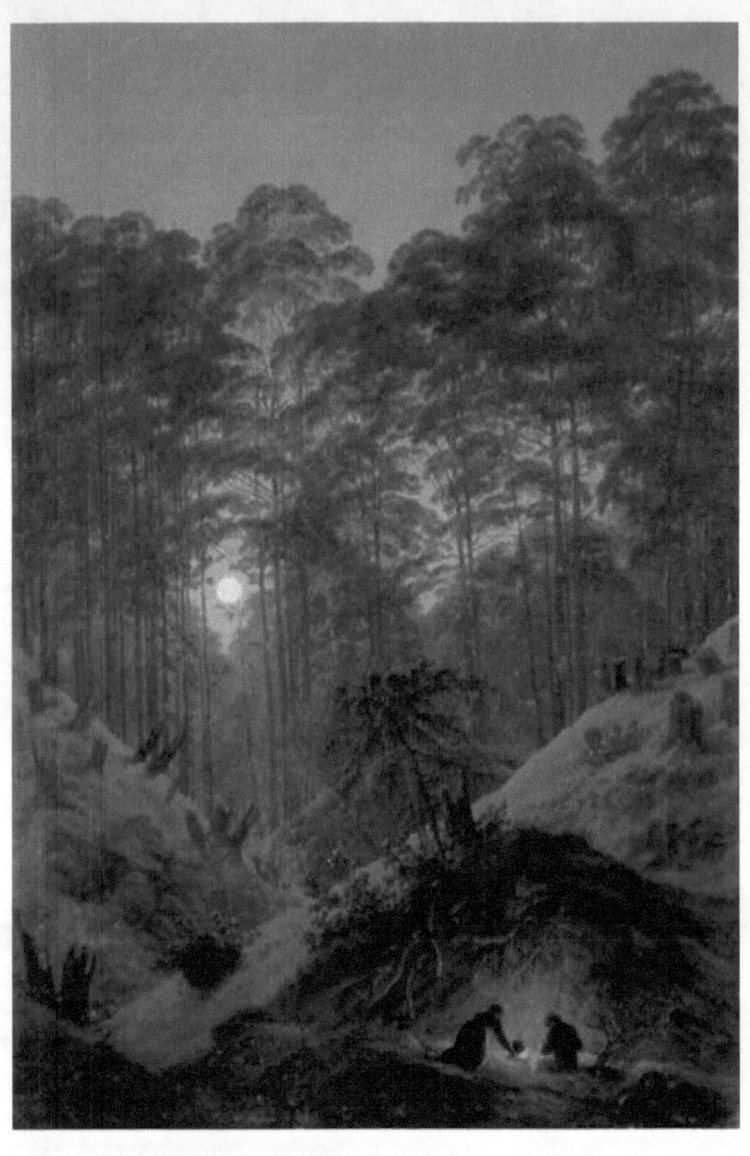

Inside the Forest under the moonlight, oil

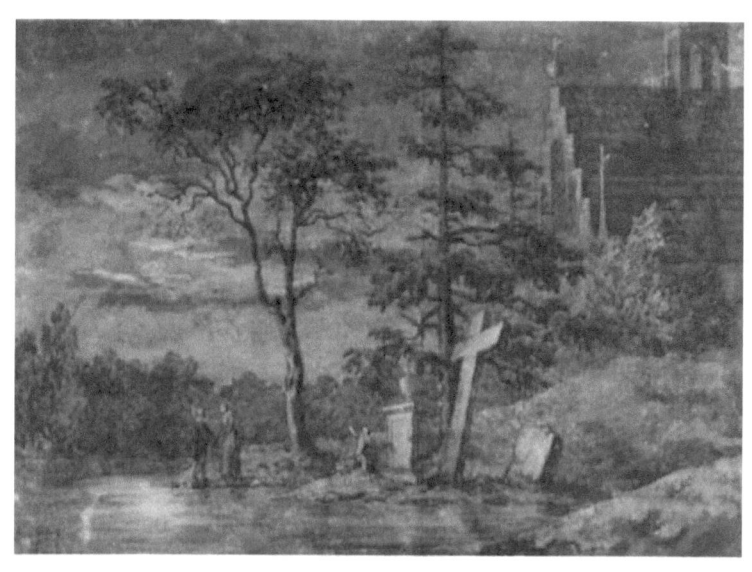

Two Men Contemplating the Moon, drawing

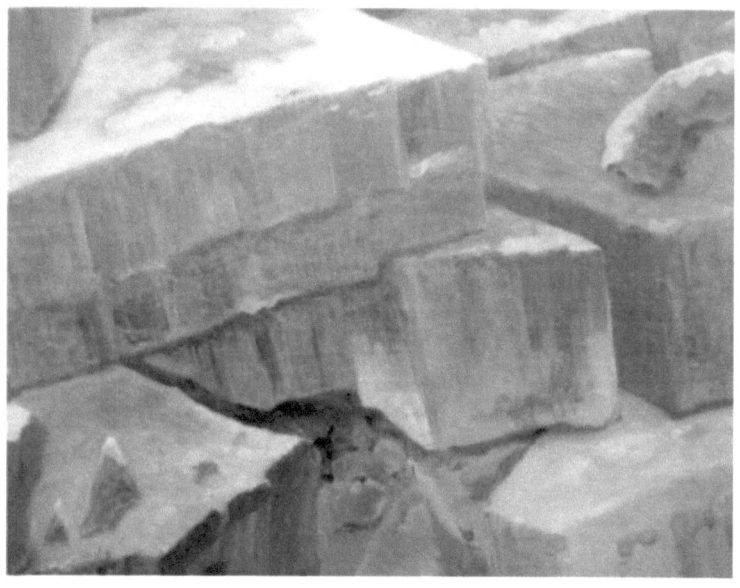

Clipping floe, oil on canvas

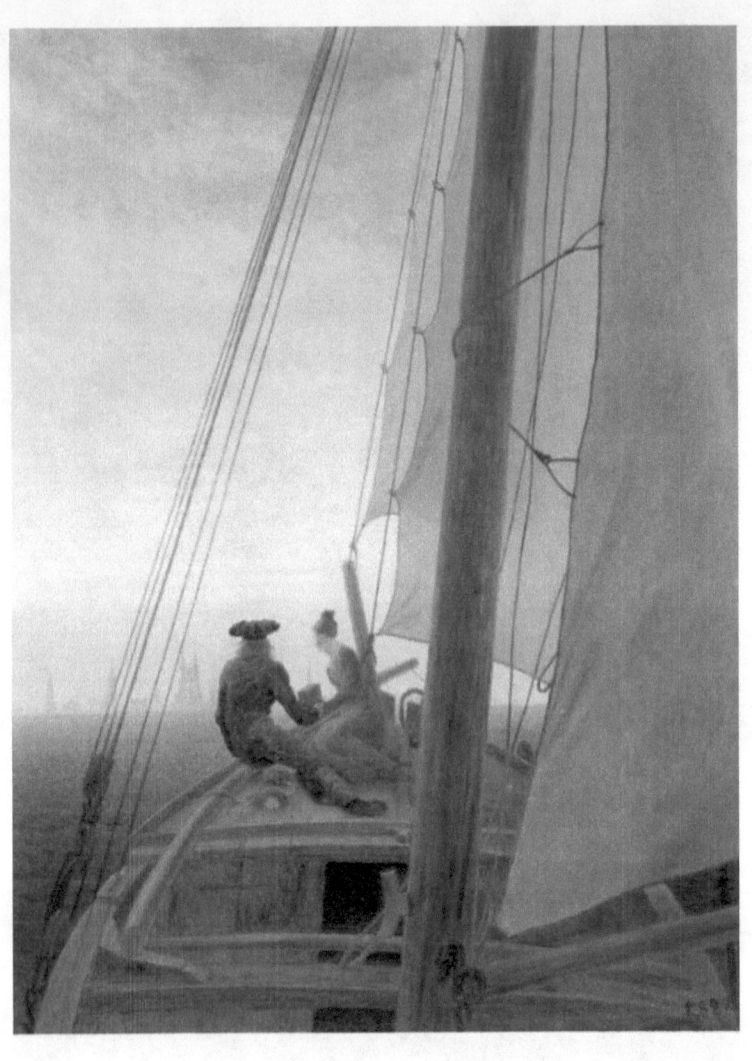

On board of a Sailing Ship, oil

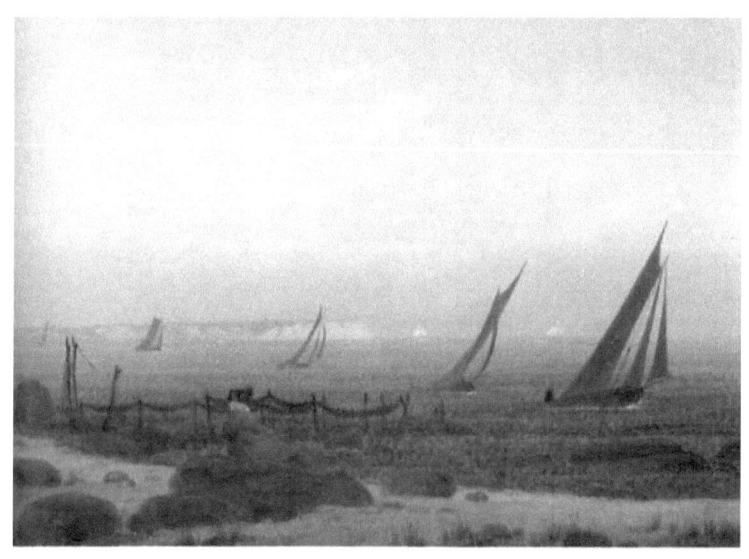

Woman on the Beach of Rugen, oil

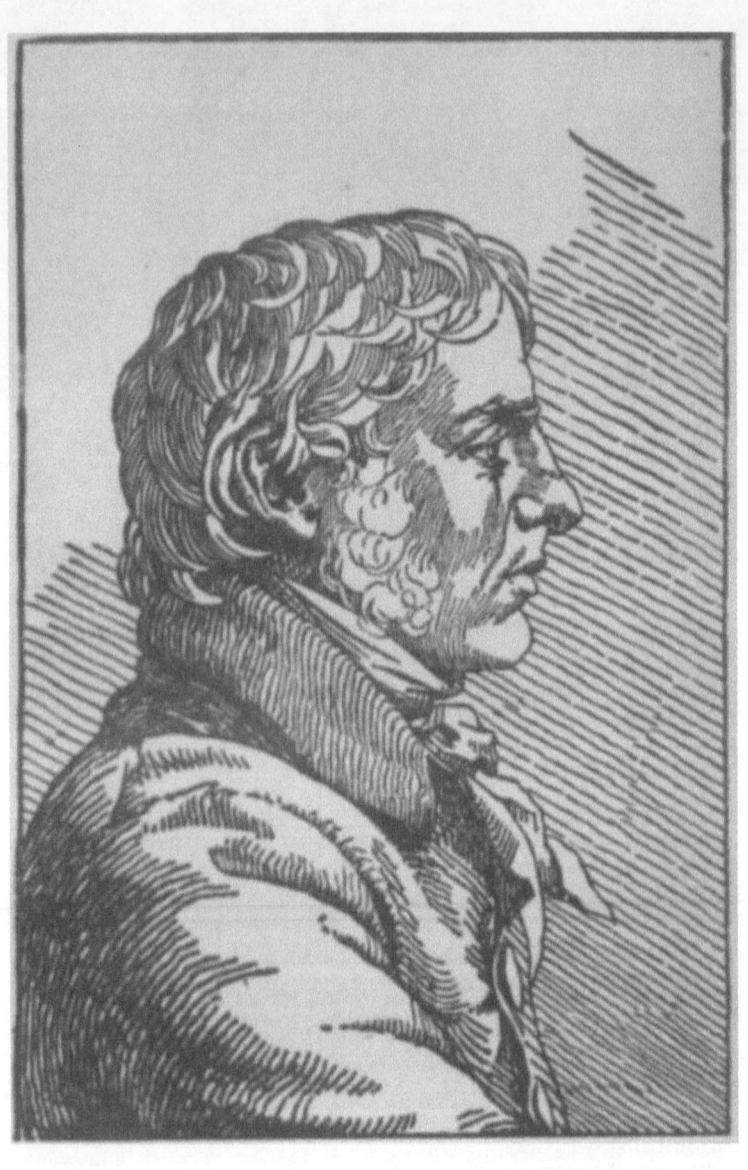

Basel, engraving

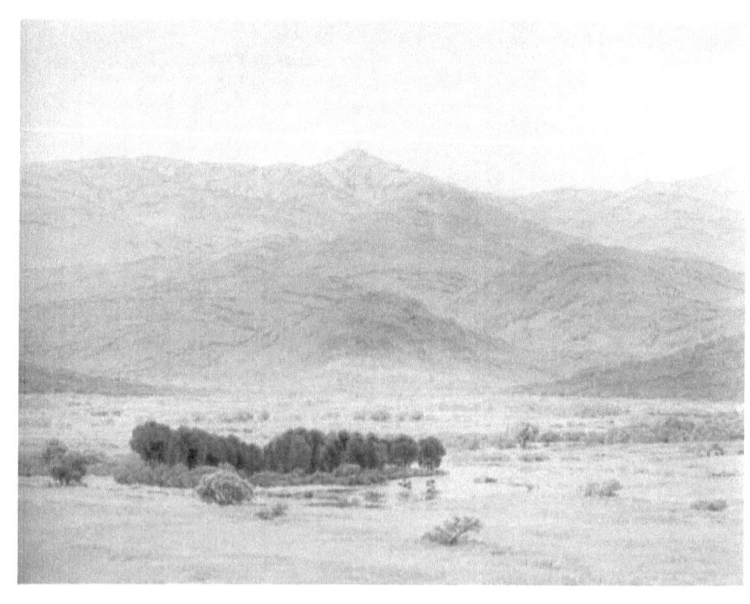

Landscape in the Riesengebirge

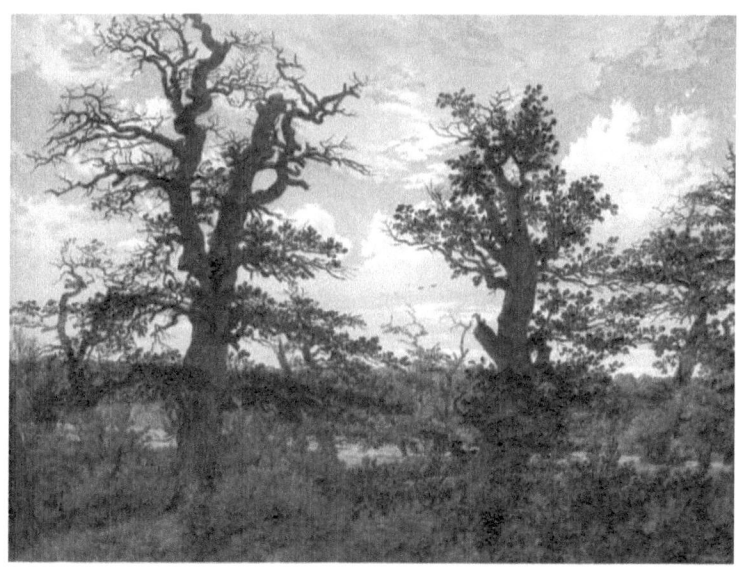

Landscape with Oak Trees and a Hunter, oil on canvas

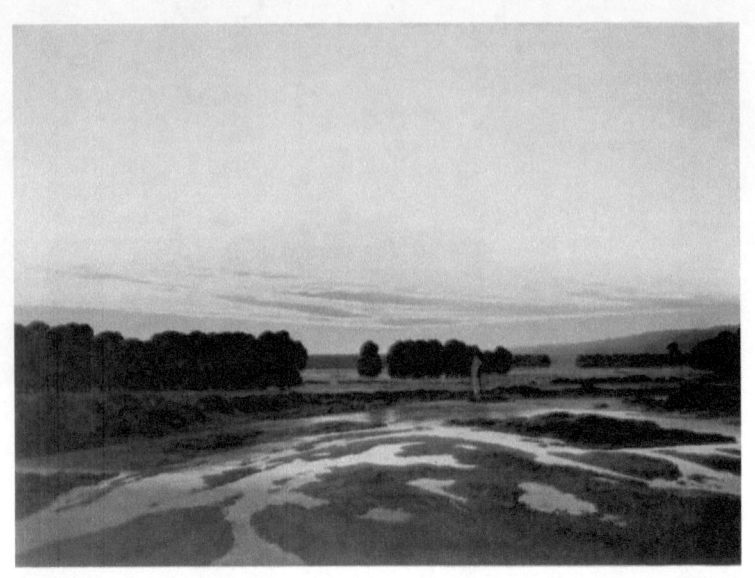

Largeness, oil on canvas

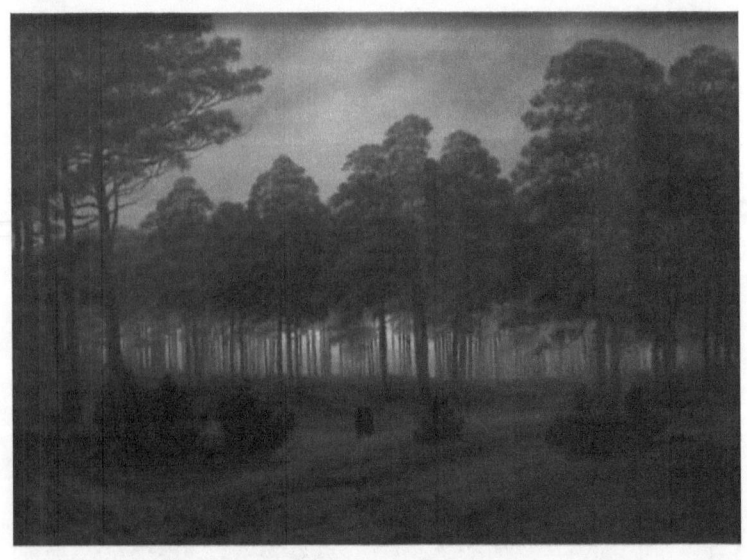

Evening, oil

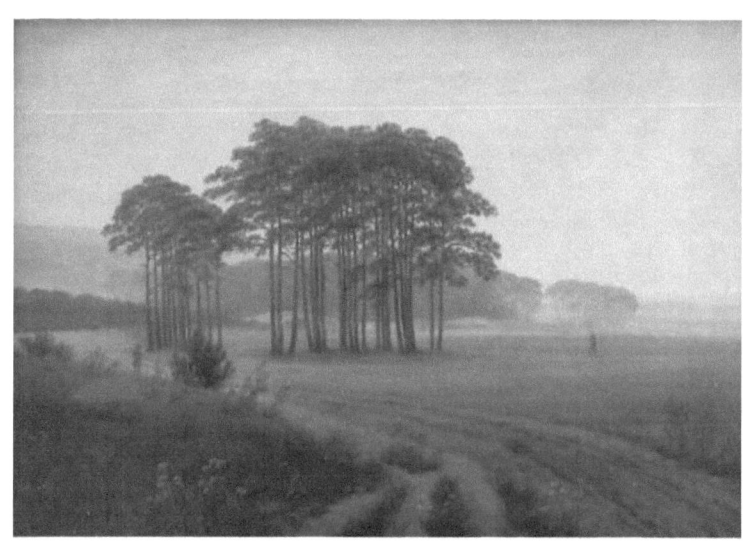

Day, oil

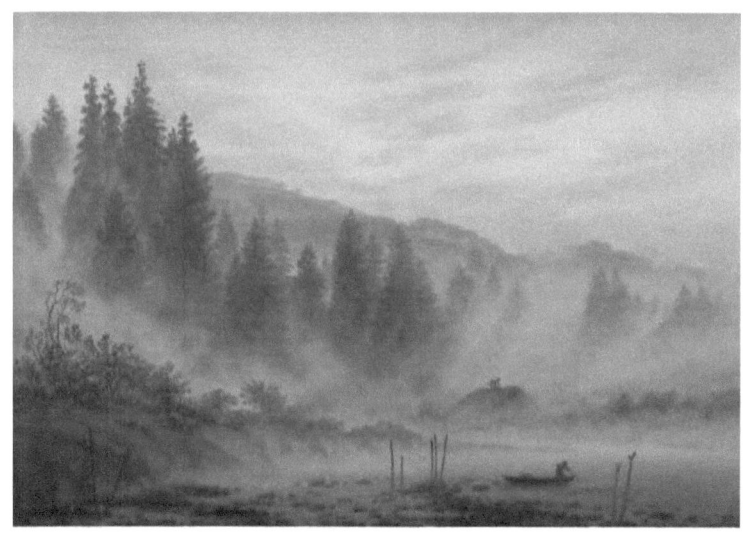

Morning, oil

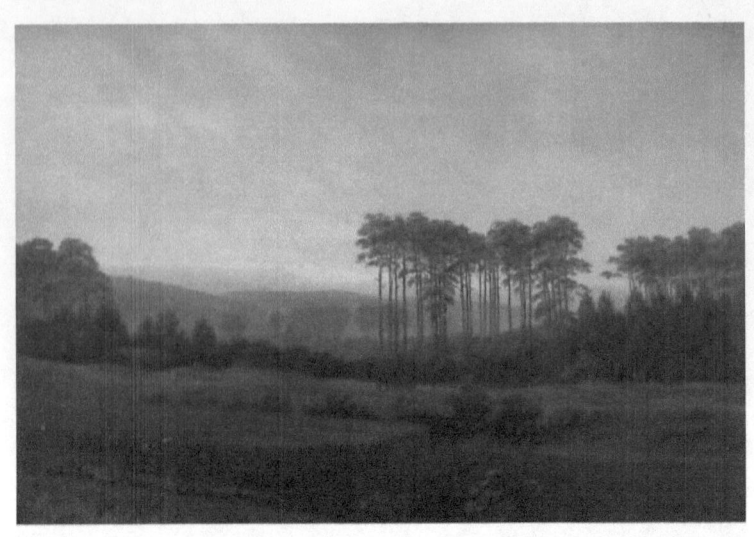

Afternoon, oil

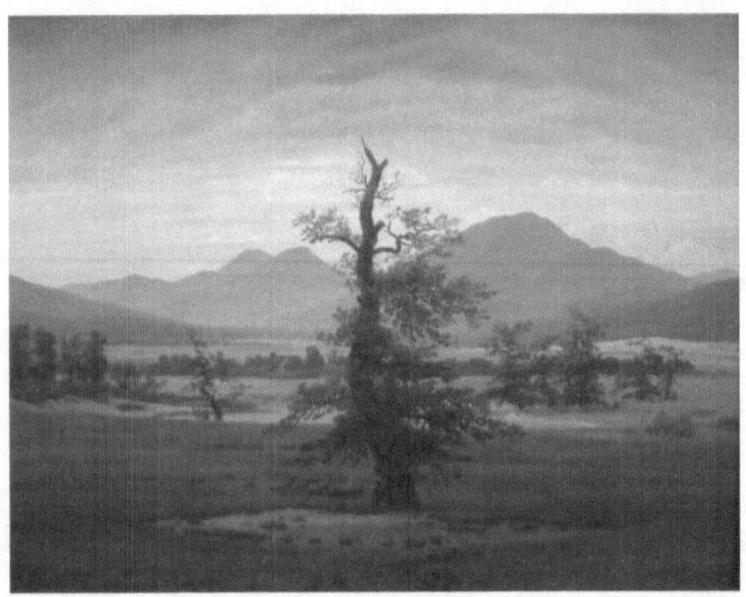

Tree, oil on canvas

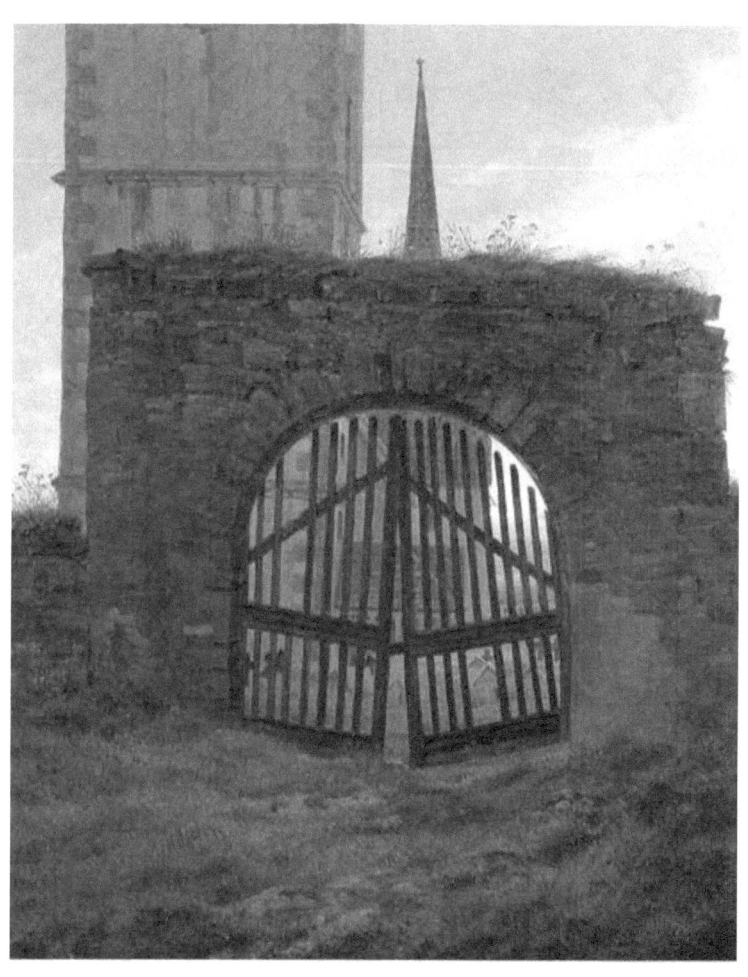

Churchyard Gate, oil

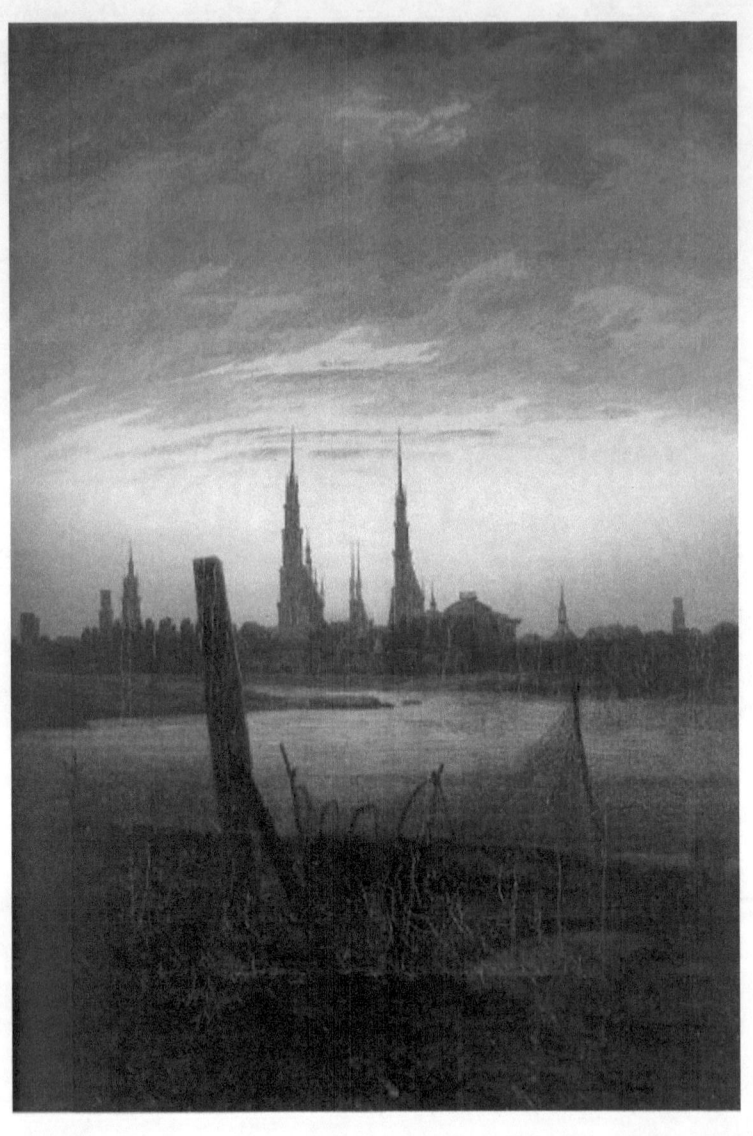

City at Moonrise, oil

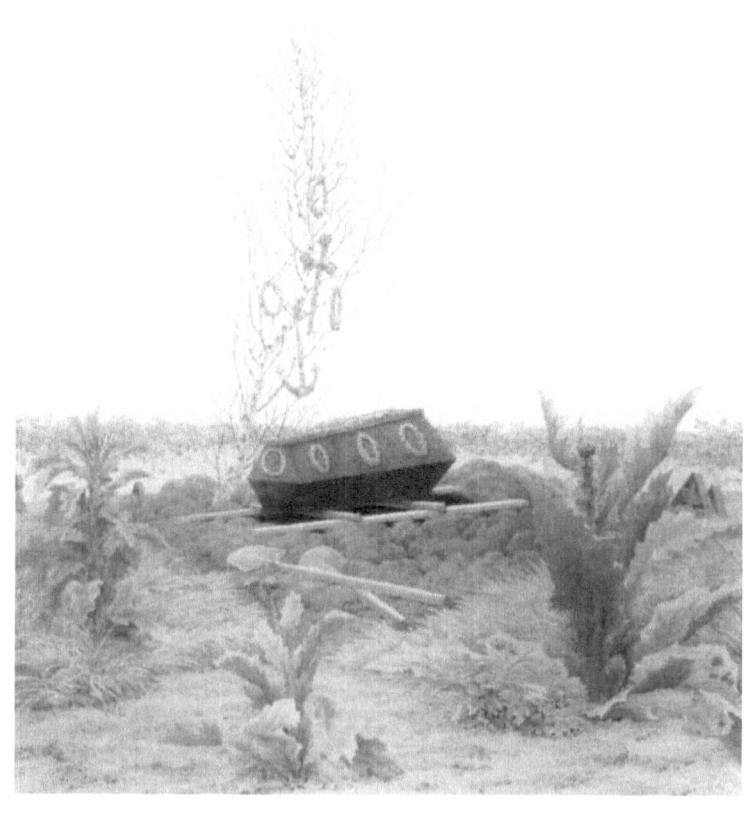

Coffin and Grave

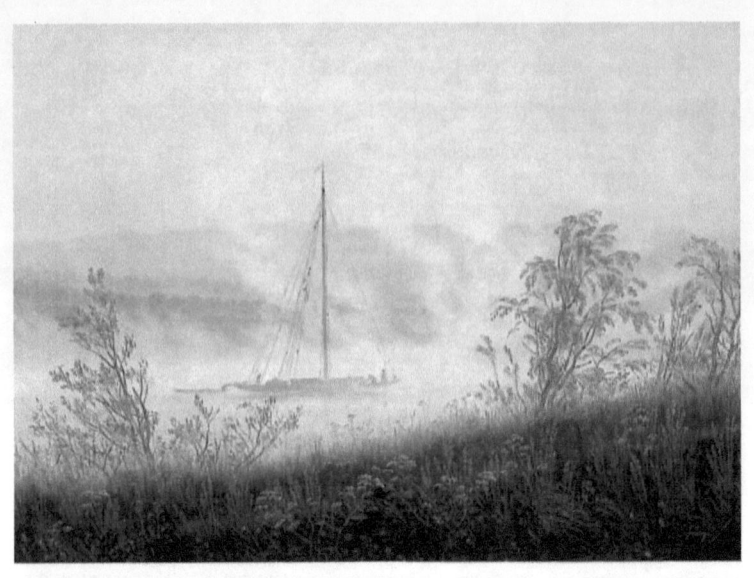

Elbschiff in early morning fog, oil on canvas

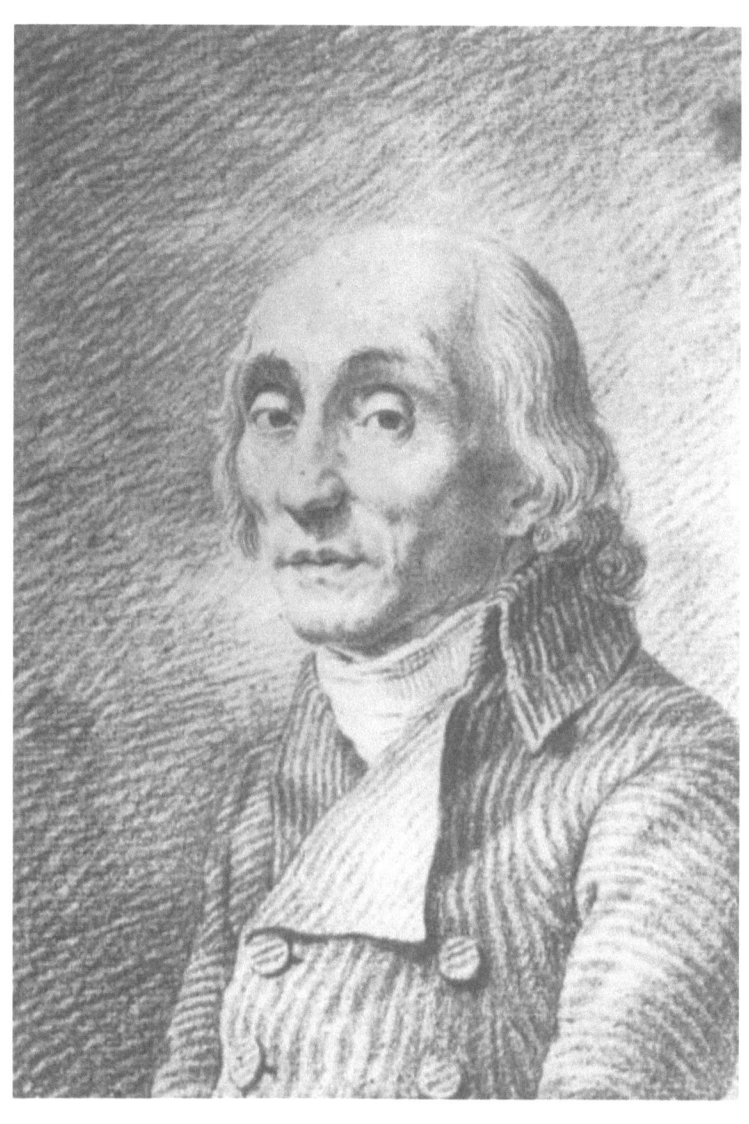

Ernst Theodor Johann Bruckner, drawing

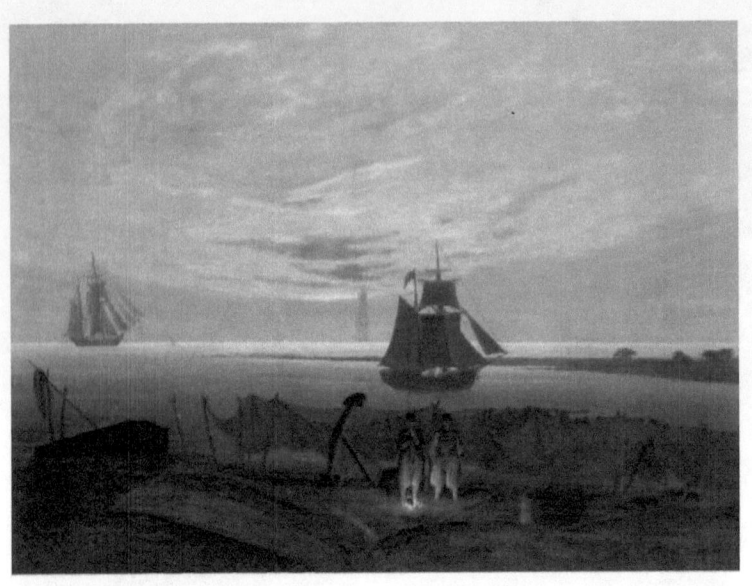

Evening on the Baltic Sea, oil

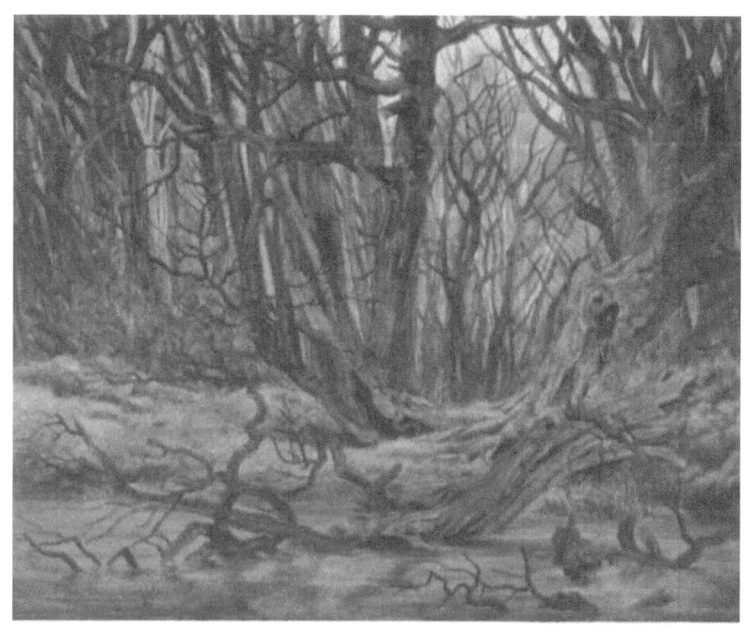

Forrest in the end of the autumn

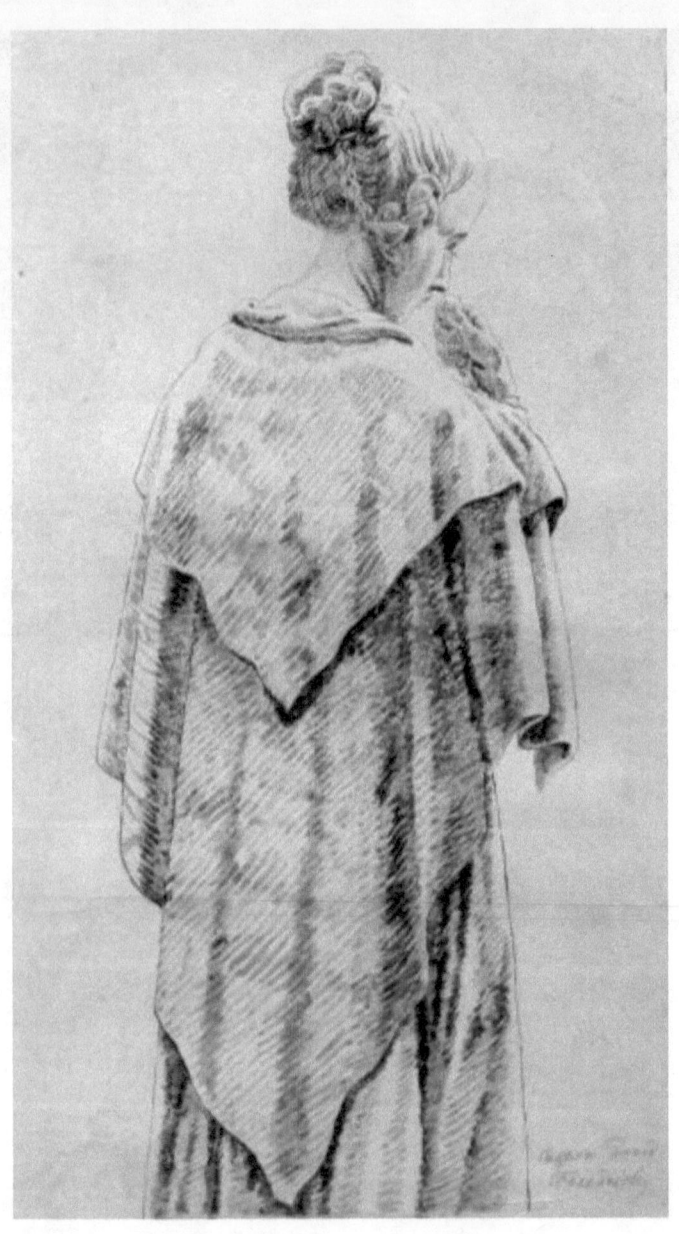

Woman in the cloack, drawing

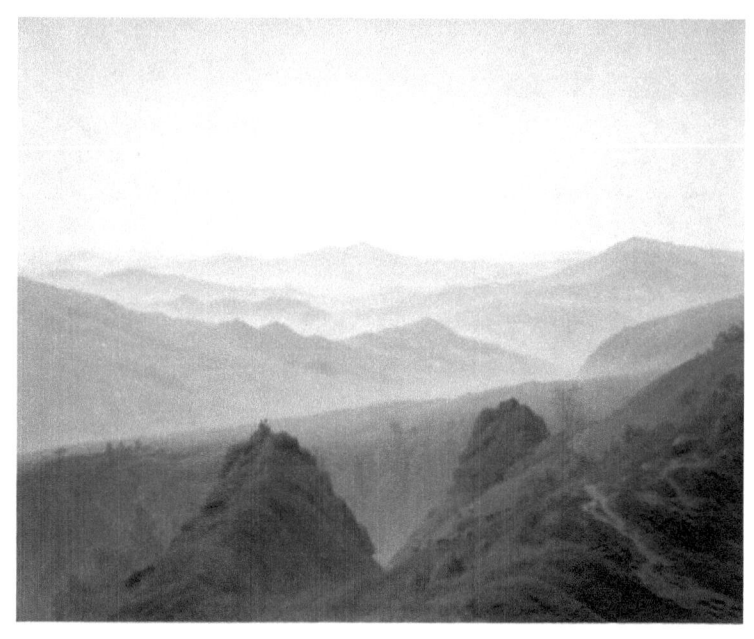

Morning in the Mountains, oil on canvas

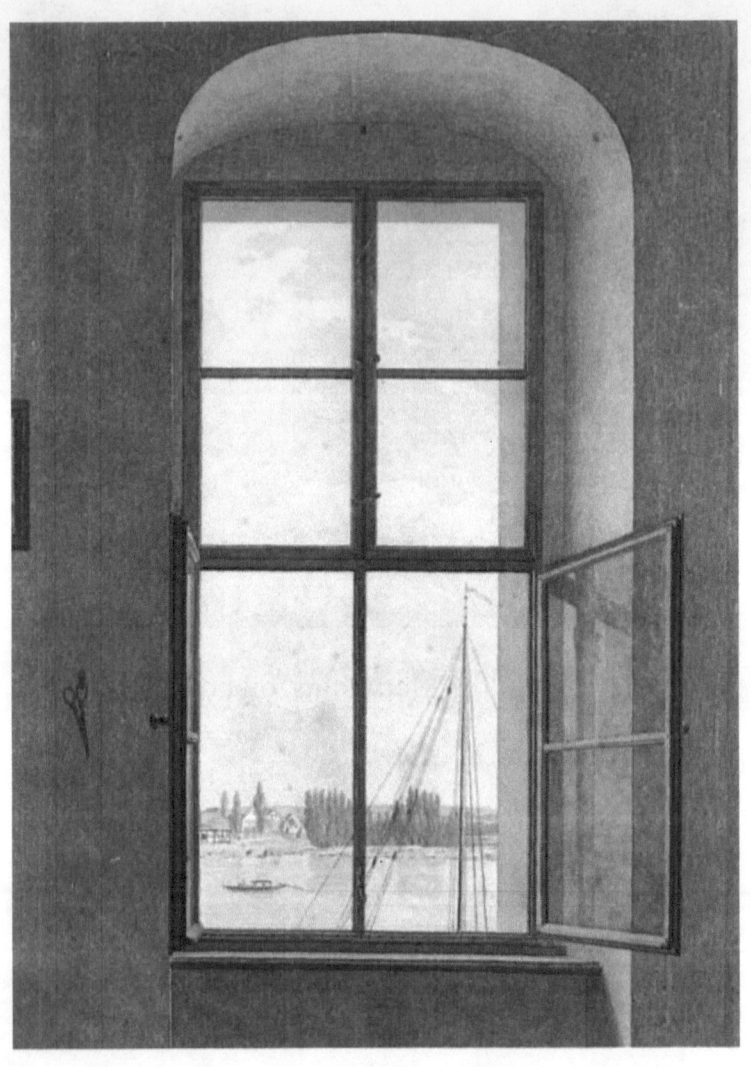

View from the Artists Studio, Window on Left

www.ingramcontent.com/pod-product-compliance
Lightning Source LLC
Chambersburg PA
CBHW020927180526
45163CB00007B/2914